THE ULTIMATE SECTION 8 WEALTH STRATEGY

A Step-by-Step Guide to Unlock Consistent Cash Flow, Build a Lucrative Real Estate Empire with Low-Income Housing and Government-Backed Tenants

Robert Newton

© Copyright 2024 - All rights reserved.

The content contained within this book may not be reproduced, duplicated, or transmitted without direct written permission from the author or the publisher.

Under no circumstances will any blame or legal responsibility be held against the publisher, or author, for any damages, reparation, or monetary loss due to the information contained within this book. Either directly or indirectly.

Legal Notice:

This book is copyright protected. This book is only for personal use. You cannot amend, distribute, sell, use, quote, or paraphrase any part, or the content within this book, without the consent of the author or publisher.

Disclaimer Notice:

By reading this document, the reader agrees that under no circumstances is the author responsible for any losses, direct or indirect, which are incurred as a result of the use of the information contained within this document, including, but not limited to, — errors, omissions, or inaccuracies.

THANK YOU
for your purchase

SCAN THIS QR CODE BELOW
to get your **FREE BONUS PLANNER** and master real estate management strategies in less than 48 hours!

Why You Shouldn't Miss This Bonus and What You'll Learn:

- **Business Strategy Planning**: Define your goals, value proposition, and action plan to build a strong foundation.
- **Financial Management**: Track revenue, expenses, and profits to stay on top of your finances.
- **Property Management Tools**: Monitor inspections, maintenance, and tenant details with ease.
- **Lead Tracking**: Keep tabs on leads and closings to grow your portfolio efficiently.

TABLE OF CONTENTS

Preface 1

Introduction 3

    The Truth About Section 8 Housing 3
    Why Section 8 Is Your Path to Wealth 6
    Getting Started: Breaking Through the Fear 6

Chapter 1: The Foundations of Section 8 Investing 12

    Understanding Section 8: How the Program Really Works ... 12
    Identifying Profitable Markets for Section 8 15
    Financing Your First Section 8 Property 17
    Navigating the Real Estate Acquisition Process 20
    Building Relationships with HUD and Local Authorities 22

Chapter 2: Preparing Your Property for Section 8 25

    Renovating with Purpose: What Matters to HUD 25
    High-ROI Repairs and Upgrades 27
    Setting Up Your Rental for Easy Maintenance 29
    The Screening Process: Choosing the Right Section 8 Tenants 31
    Passing Inspections with Ease 34

Chapter 3: Managing Section 8 Tenants Like a Pro 36

    Running Your Properties Like a Business 36
    Mastering Tenant Relations 38

    Avoiding the "Tenant from Hell" 40
    Streamlining Rent Collection 42
    Dealing with Evictions and Legal Issues 44

Chapter 4: Scaling Your Section 8 Empire 47

    When and How to Expand Your Portfolio 47
    Multi-Unit Properties: The Pros and Cons 49
    Funding Your Growth 51
    Building a Team of Experts 53
    Diversifying Your Real Estate Holdings 55

Chapter 5: Advanced Property Management Techniques 58

    Effective Cost Management 58
    Staying Ahead of Inspections 60
    Tenant Retention Strategies 62
    Leveraging Technology in Property Management 64
    Dealing with Unexpected Challenges 66

Chapter 6: The Legal Side of Section 8 Investing 68

    Understanding Your Legal Responsibilities 68
    Crafting Bulletproof Leases 70
    Avoiding Legal Pitfalls 72
    How to Handle Tenant Disputes 74
    Insurance and Liability Protection 75

Chapter 7: Handling Difficult Tenants and Situations 78

    Dealing with Non-Paying Tenants 78
    Evicting Problem Tenants 80
    Tenant Damage Control 82
    Handling Tenant Complaints and Disputes 84
    Safety Measures for Landlords 86

Chapter 8: Strategic Property Maintenance 88

Low-Cost, High-Impact Repairs 88
Preventative Maintenance Tips 90
Finding Reliable Contractors 91
Budgeting for Repairs and Maintenance 93
Implementing Green Upgrades for Savings 95

Chapter 9: Mastering the Financials of Section 8 Investing . 97

Maximizing Cash Flow from Section 8 Rentals 97
Tracking Your Real Estate Profits 99
Understanding Tax Benefits and Incentives 100
Leveraging Depreciation and Write-Offs 102
Creating Long-Term Wealth through Real Estate 104

Chapter 10: Section 8 Inspections and Compliance 106

Preparing for HUD Inspections 106
Dealing with Inspection Failures 108
Building Relationships with Inspectors 110
Keeping Your Properties Compliant Year-Round 111
Handling Emergency Repairs 113

Chapter 11: Exit Strategies and Long-Term Planning 115

When to Sell Your Section 8 Properties 115
Selling Your Portfolio for Maximum Profit 117
Tax Planning for Property Sales 118
Transitioning from Active to Passive Investing 120
Leaving a Legacy: Building Wealth for Generations 122

Chapter 12: Street-Smart Tips for Section 8 Landlords 124

Safety Tips for Working in High-Crime Areas 124

Playing Fair but Firm with Tenants 126
Dealing with Difficult Inspectors and Bureaucrats 128
Handling Legal Challenges and Court Cases 130
The Long Game: Lessons from a Veteran Investor 132

Conclusion 134

PREFACE

Real estate investing has long been recognized as a powerful vehicle for building wealth and financial freedom. However, the path to success in this field is often shrouded in mystery, with many potential investors intimidated by the perceived complexities and risks. This is particularly true when it comes to Section 8 housing—a sector that, despite its potential for consistent and reliable income, is often overlooked due to misunderstandings and misconceptions.

As an experienced real estate investor and author, I've spent years navigating the ins and outs of the Section 8 program. I've experienced firsthand the challenges, triumphs, and lucrative rewards that this unique niche has to offer. And now, I'm eager to share my insights and strategies with you in this comprehensive guide: The Ultimate Section 8 Wealth Strategy: A Step-by-Step Guide to Unlock Consistent Cash Flow, Build a Lucrative Real Estate Empire with Low-Income Housing and Government-Backed Tenants.

Robert Newton

This book is designed to demystify the Section 8 program and provide you with a clear, step-by-step blueprint for success. Whether you're a novice investor seeking a low-barrier entry point into real estate, an experienced landlord looking to diversify your portfolio, or a real estate professional eager to master a profitable niche, this book will equip you with the knowledge and tools you need to thrive.

We'll start by laying a solid foundation, explaining how the Section 8 program works, and why it represents such a compelling opportunity for investors. We'll then delve into the practicalities of acquiring and preparing properties, screening tenants, and passing HUD inspections.

But this book is about more than just the nuts and bolts of Section 8 investing. It's about empowering you to build a scalable real estate portfolio, manage properties efficiently, and navigate the legal landscape confidently. It's about sharing street-smart tips and strategies to handle difficult tenants, maximize cash flow, and leverage tax benefits. And ultimately, it's about helping you to create long-term wealth and financial freedom through real estate.

Throughout this journey, I'll be right there with you, sharing my own experiences, successes, and lessons learned. My goal is not just to inform, but to inspire—to show you that if I can do it, so can you.

So, are you ready to unlock the power of Section 8 investing and take your first steps towards building a lucrative real estate empire? If so, let's get started. The road to financial freedom awaits.

Robert Newton

INTRODUCTION

The Truth About Section 8 Housing

Welcome to the world of Section 8 investing—a realm that, despite its potential for consistent and reliable income, is often overlooked due to misunderstandings and misconceptions. So, let's begin by dispelling some of the myths and revealing the truth about Section 8 housing.

Section 8, officially known as the Housing Choice Voucher Program, is a federal assistance program designed to help low-income families, the elderly, and the disabled afford safe and decent housing in the private market. It's administered by local public housing agencies (PHAs) under the oversight of the U.S. Department of Housing and Urban Development (HUD).

Now, let's address the elephant in the room: the stigma attached to Section 8 housing. Many investors shy away from Section 8 due to the stereotype of problem tenants and the perceived hassle of dealing with government bureaucracy. While these concerns are not entirely unfounded, they often stem from a lack of understanding or experience.

In reality, Section 8 tenants come from a variety of backgrounds, just like any other renters. Yes, some may pose challenges, but so can tenants in any other rental situation. The key is in your tenant screening process, which we'll delve into in later chapters. As for the government red tape, while there are indeed regulations and inspections to comply with, these can be navigated smoothly with the right knowledge and preparation.

Now, let's talk about the benefits. The most significant advantage of Section 8 investing is the consistent, government-backed rent payments. Each month, a portion of the rent is paid directly to the landlord by the PHA, reducing the risk of late or missed payments. This can provide a steady cash flow, making it an attractive option for investors seeking reliable income.

Moreover, because the demand for affordable housing often exceeds the supply, vacancy rates for Section 8 properties tend to be lower than the market average. This means less time and money spent on advertising and showing your property, and more time enjoying your passive income.

Another often-overlooked benefit of Section 8 investing is the potential for higher rents. In many areas, the PHA's payment standards (the maximum amount they'll pay for rent and utilities) are competitive with, or even higher than, market rents. This means you can earn a fair return on your investment while providing much-needed housing for low-income families.

But perhaps the most compelling reason to consider Section 8 investing is its potential for impact. By providing quality housing to low-income families, you're not just building wealth for yourself; you're also making a positive difference in your community. This sense of purpose can be incredibly rewarding and can add a layer of meaning to your investment strategy that goes beyond dollars and cents.

Of course, like any investment, Section 8 housing is not without its challenges. There will be hurdles to overcome, from navigating HUD regulations to dealing with difficult tenants. But with the right mindset, knowledge, and strategies—which I'll provide in this book—these challenges can be managed and even turned into opportunities.

Breaking into Section 8 investing may seem daunting, especially if you're new to real estate. But let me assure you: it's not as complex as it might seem. With the right guidance and a willingness to learn, anyone can succeed in this niche. So, let's set aside any fears or doubts you may have. You're about to embark on an exciting journey—one that could lead you to financial freedom and beyond.

So, are you ready to uncover the truth about Section 8 housing and unlock its wealth-building potential? If so, let's dive in. The world of Section 8 investing awaits.

Why Section 8 Is Your Path to Wealth

Now that we've cleared the air on some of the common misconceptions about Section 8 housing, let's delve into why this program could be your golden ticket to wealth.

First, let's talk about the consistent, government-backed income. As a Section 8 landlord, you're not just relying on your tenant's ability to pay rent each month. A significant portion of your rental income comes directly from the government. This means that even in times of economic uncertainty, you have a steady stream of income. In fact, during economic downturns, when many people are struggling financially, the demand for Section 8 housing often increases, providing even more potential tenants.

Next, consider the size of the market. Millions of families in the U.S. rely on Section 8 housing. This vast pool of potential tenants can provide a higher occupancy rate for your properties. Higher occupancy rates mean fewer vacancies, and fewer vacancies mean more consistent income.

But the benefits of Section 8 investing extend beyond steady income and high demand. There's also the potential for above-market rent. The PHAs determine a payment standard that is the maximum amount they will pay for each unit size. This amount is based on the fair market rent in your area. In some cases, this payment standard can be higher than the going rate for similar units in your area, allowing you to collect more rent than you might otherwise be able to.

Section 8 also offers the opportunity for social impact. By providing quality housing for low-income families, you're playing a part in addressing a critical social issue. This aspect of Section 8 investing is often overlooked but can be a rewarding part of the process.

Now, let's address the wealth-building aspect of Section 8 investing. Real estate is a tried-and-true wealth builder. It's a tangible asset that, over time, tends to appreciate in value. As a landlord, you're not only collecting rent each month, but you're also building equity in your property. This equity can be leveraged to expand your real estate portfolio and multiply your wealth.

Moreover, real estate offers tax advantages that can further enhance your wealth-building efforts. As a property owner, you can deduct certain expenses related to owning and managing your property, such as mortgage interest, property taxes, insurance, maintenance costs, and more. These deductions can significantly reduce your taxable income, allowing you to keep more of your hard-earned money.

But perhaps one of the most compelling reasons why Section 8 is a path to wealth is the scalability of the model. Once you've navigated the process with one property, you can replicate it with additional properties. With each new property, you add another stream of consistent, government-backed income, accelerating your wealth-building journey.

Of course, scaling a real estate portfolio involves managing more properties, dealing with more tenants, and juggling more responsibilities. But with the right systems in place, which we'll discuss in later chapters, you can manage a large portfolio efficiently and even outsource many of the day-to-day tasks.

In essence, Section 8 investing can provide a steady income, a high demand market, potential for above-market rent, opportunities for social impact, wealth-building through property appreciation and tax benefits, and a scalable business model. All these factors combined make it a compelling path to wealth.

But as we've discussed, Section 8 investing is not without its challenges. It requires a willingness to navigate government regulations, manage tenant relationships, and maintain properties to meet HUD standards. It's not a get-rich-quick scheme, but a strategic approach to building wealth over time.

In the next section, we'll discuss how to get started with Section 8 investing, breaking through the fear and taking the first steps towards building your real estate empire. As we move forward, remember that every successful investor started where you are now, at the beginning. With knowledge, persistence, and a bit of courage, you too can build wealth through Section 8 investing.

Getting Started: Breaking Through the Fear

As we delve deeper into the world of Section 8 investing, it's natural to feel a sense of trepidation. After all, real estate investing—like any business venture—comes with its share of risks and uncertainties. But let me assure you: breaking through this initial fear is one of the most crucial steps towards achieving your financial goals.

Fear is a natural human response to the unknown. It's our brain's way of protecting us from perceived threats. But while this instinct can be useful in certain situations, it can also hold us back from seizing valuable opportunities. In the realm of real estate investing, fear often takes the form of doubts and 'what ifs.' What if I choose the wrong property? What if I can't find good tenants? What if the market crashes?

These are valid concerns, and it's important to approach investing with a healthy dose of caution. However, it's equally important not to let fear paralyze you into inaction. The truth is, every successful investor has faced these same fears at some point. The difference is that they chose to confront them head-on, armed with knowledge, preparation, and a solid plan.

So, how do you break through the fear and take the leap into Section 8 investing? It starts with education. Knowledge is a powerful antidote to fear. The more you understand about the Section 8 program, the real estate market, and the principles of investing, the more confident you'll feel in your ability to navigate the challenges and seize the opportunities.

That's where this book comes in. Consider it your roadmap to success in Section 8 investing. In the following chapters, we'll delve into the practicalities of acquiring and managing properties, navigating HUD regulations, screening tenants, and more. We'll also explore strategies for building a scalable real estate portfolio, maximizing cash flow, and protecting yourself legally.

But knowledge alone is not enough. To truly conquer your fears, you must also cultivate the right mindset. This means embracing the challenges as opportunities for growth, staying adaptable in the face of change, and maintaining a relentless focus on your long-term goals.

Remember, every successful investor started where you are now. They faced the same fears, the same uncertainties, and the same steep learning curve. But they didn't let that stop them. They pushed through the fear, took the leap, and reaped the rewards. And with the right knowledge, mindset, and guidance, you can do the same.

One of the most effective ways to overcome fear is to take action. Start small, perhaps with a single property, and learn as you go. Each step you take will build your confidence, broaden your experience, and bring you closer to your financial goals.

Finally, remember that you're not alone in this journey. There are countless resources available to help you succeed, from real estate investing forums and networking groups to mentors and coaches. Don't be afraid to seek help and learn from those who have walked the path before you.

In the end, breaking through the fear is not about eliminating risks or uncertainties—it's about learning to manage them effectively. It's about equipping yourself with the knowledge, skills, and mindset to turn challenges into opportunities. And most importantly, it's about taking that first step towards building wealth and financial freedom through Section 8 investing.

So, are you ready to confront your fears and take the leap into the exciting world of Section 8 investing? If so, let's continue our journey. The road to wealth and financial freedom awaits.

Chapter 1

THE FOUNDATIONS OF SECTION 8 INVESTING

Understanding Section 8: How the Program Really Works

As we embark on this journey into the world of Section 8 investing, it's crucial to start with a solid understanding of the program itself. After all, the more you understand about how Section 8 works, the better equipped you'll be to leverage its benefits and navigate its challenges. So, let's take a closer look at the inner workings of the Section 8 program.

Section 8, officially known as the Housing Choice Voucher Program, is a federal assistance program designed to help low-income families, the elderly, and the disabled afford safe and decent housing in the private market. It's administered by local public housing agencies (PHAs) under the oversight of the U.S. Department of Housing and Urban Development (HUD).

The program works by issuing housing vouchers to eligible tenants, who then find a suitable housing unit—like your rental property—where the landlord agrees to rent under the program. Once the tenant moves in, the PHA pays a housing subsidy directly to the landlord, with the tenant paying the difference.

The amount of the subsidy is based on a variety of factors, including the tenant's income, the size of the family, and the rental market in the area. The tenant's portion of the rent is typically around 30% of their monthly adjusted gross income, with the PHA paying the rest.

One of the unique aspects of Section 8 is the inspection process. Before a property can be rented to a Section 8 tenant, it must pass a HUD Housing Quality Standards (HQS) inspection conducted by the PHA. The property must also pass annual inspections to remain in the program. While this may seem like a hassle, it's actually an opportunity to ensure your property is well-maintained and attractive to tenants.

Now, let's talk about the benefits from an investor's perspective. The most obvious advantage is the consistent, government-backed rent payments. As a landlord, you'll receive a portion of the rent directly from the PHA each month, reducing the risk of late or missed payments. This can provide a steady cash flow, which is the lifeblood of any successful real estate investment.

Another advantage is the potential for lower vacancy rates. Because the demand for affordable housing often exceeds the supply,

Section 8 properties tend to have lower vacancy rates than the market average. This means less time and money spent on advertising and showing your property, and more time enjoying your passive income.

Moreover, the PHA's payment standards—the maximum amount they'll pay for rent and utilities—are often competitive with, or even higher than, market rents. This means you can potentially earn a fair return on your investment while providing much-needed housing for low-income families.

But perhaps the most compelling reason to consider Section 8 investing is its potential for impact. By providing quality housing to low-income families, you're not just building wealth for yourself; you're also making a positive difference in your community. This sense of purpose can add a layer of meaning to your investment strategy that goes beyond dollars and cents.

Like any investment, Section 8 housing is not without its challenges. There will be hurdles to overcome, from navigating HUD regulations to dealing with difficult tenants. But with the right mindset, knowledge, and strategies—which I'll provide in this book—these challenges can be managed and even turned into opportunities.

In the following chapters, we'll delve deeper into the practicalities of Section 8 investing, from acquiring and preparing properties to screening tenants and passing HUD inspections. We'll also explore strategies for building a scalable real estate portfolio, managing properties efficiently, and navigating the legal landscape.

But for now, I hope this overview has given you a clearer understanding of how the Section 8 program works and why it represents such a compelling opportunity for investors. As we move forward, keep this information in mind. It will serve as the foundation for everything else we'll cover in this book.

So, are you ready to dive deeper into the world of Section 8 investing? If so, let's continue our journey. The path to wealth and financial freedom awaits.

Identifying Profitable Markets for Section 8

Now that we've laid out the basics of the Section 8 program, let's delve into one of the most critical aspects of real estate investing: market selection. Identifying profitable markets for Section 8 housing is an art and science that requires careful research, strategic thinking, and a deep understanding of local housing trends.

The first step in identifying profitable markets is understanding the demand for affordable housing in different areas. In general, areas with high rental rates and low vacancy rates tend to be good markets for Section 8 housing. This is because the demand for affordable housing often outstrips the supply, leading to lower vacancy rates and higher rents for Section 8 properties.

However, it's not enough to simply look at rental rates and vacancy rates. You also need to consider the local economy, job market, population trends, and other factors that can influence the demand for housing. For instance, areas with strong job growth, a growing population, and a lack of affordable housing options are often ripe for Section 8 investing.

Another key factor to consider is the local PHA's payment standards. These are the maximum amounts that the PHA will pay for rent and utilities for different sizes of housing units. In many areas, these payment standards are competitive with, or even higher than, market rents. By investing in areas with high payment standards, you can potentially earn a higher return on your investment.

Once you've identified potential markets, the next step is to conduct a detailed analysis of each market. This involves researching local housing trends, studying the local economy, and talking to local real estate professionals and PHA officials. The goal is to gain a deep understanding of the local housing market and the potential opportunities for Section 8 investing.

One useful tool for conducting market analysis is the U.S. Department of Housing and Urban Development's (HUD's) Fair Market Rents (FMRs). These are estimates of the average rents in a particular area for different types of housing units. By comparing the FMRs with the actual rents in the area, you can get a sense of the potential profitability of Section 8 properties.

Another important part of market selection is building relationships with local PHAs. These agencies administer the Section 8 program and can provide valuable insights into the local housing market. They can also help you navigate the Section 8 program and understand the local regulations and requirements.

Finally, remember that market selection is not a one-time process. Markets can change over time due to economic trends, changes in government policy, and other factors. Therefore, it's important to continually monitor your chosen markets and be ready to adapt your strategy as needed.

Identifying profitable markets for Section 8 housing is not about finding the "perfect" market. It's about understanding the dynamics of different markets, making informed decisions, and being willing to adapt and learn as you go. With careful research, strategic thinking, and a deep understanding of the Section 8 program, you can identify profitable markets and seize the opportunities they offer.

So, are you ready to start identifying profitable markets for Section 8 housing? If so, let's continue our journey. The path to wealth and financial freedom awaits.

Financing Your First Section 8 Property

Securing financing is often one of the most challenging aspects of real estate investing, especially for newcomers. However, it's also one of the most critical steps in the process. Without adequate financing, even the most promising investment opportunity can quickly become unfeasible. So, let's delve into the nuts and bolts of financing your first Section 8 property.

The first thing to understand about financing a Section 8 property is that it's not fundamentally different from financing any other type of real estate investment. The same basic options are available: you can use cash, secure a mortgage, or explore alternative financing methods like private lenders or real estate crowdfunding platforms.

However, there are a few unique aspects to consider when financing a Section 8 property. One of these is the potential impact of the Section 8 program on your loan approval process. Some lenders may view Section 8 properties as riskier due to the perceived challenges of dealing with low-income tenants or government regulations. However, others may see the guaranteed government-backed rent payments as a plus.

When seeking financing, it's crucial to work with a lender who understands the Section 8 program and is comfortable with this type of investment. This might be a traditional bank, a credit union, or a mortgage broker. Don't be afraid to shop around and compare terms from different lenders to find the best deal.

Another important consideration is the type of loan you choose. For most investors, a conventional mortgage will be the most straightforward option. These loans typically require a down payment of 20% or more, although some lenders may offer loans with lower down payments. Keep in mind that the lower your down payment, the higher your monthly mortgage payments will be.

If you're a first-time homebuyer, you might be eligible for special loan programs with lower down payment requirements or other benefits. For instance, the Federal Housing Administration (FHA) offers loans with down payments as low as 3.5% for first-time buyers. Similarly, the Department of Veterans Affairs (VA) offers loans with no down payment for eligible veterans and service members.

For those looking to invest in multi-family properties, the FHA also offers a loan program specifically for this purpose. The FHA 203(k) loan allows investors to finance both the purchase and rehabilitation of a property with a single loan. This can be a great option if you're looking to invest in a property that needs significant repairs to meet HUD's Housing Quality Standards.

In addition to these traditional financing options, there are also several alternative financing methods to consider. These include private money lenders, hard money loans, and real estate crowdfunding platforms. While these options can offer more flexibility, they often come with higher interest rates and shorter repayment terms, so be sure to weigh the pros and cons carefully.

Finally, remember that financing is just one piece of the puzzle. In addition to securing financing, you'll also need to budget for other expenses like property inspections, closing costs, property management fees, and ongoing maintenance and repairs. Be sure to factor these costs into your financial planning to ensure a profitable investment.

In the end, financing your first Section 8 property is a significant step on your journey to financial freedom. It may seem daunting at first, but with careful planning, diligent research, and a solid understanding of your financing options, you can secure the funding you need to make your real estate investing dreams a reality.

So, are you ready to take the next step in your Section 8 investing journey? If so, let's continue our journey. The path to wealth and financial freedom awaits.

Navigating the Real Estate Acquisition Process

Now that we've tackled the financial aspect of investing in Section 8 properties, let's move on to another vital component of your investment journey: the acquisition process. Acquiring a property is more than just a financial transaction; it's a strategic move that can set the stage for your success (or failure) as a real estate investor.

The first step in the acquisition process is identifying potential properties. This involves researching the local real estate market, visiting properties, and evaluating their potential as Section 8 rentals. Remember, not all properties are suitable for the Section 8 program. The property must meet HUD's Housing Quality Standards, and the rent must be within the local PHA's payment standards.

Once you've identified a potential property, the next step is to make an offer. This is where your negotiation skills come into play. It's important to strike a balance between offering a price that's attractive to the seller and ensuring that the deal makes financial sense for you. Don't be afraid to negotiate on price, terms, or even repairs.

After your offer is accepted, it's time for due diligence. This is a critical phase where you verify the condition of the property, review any leases or tenant agreements, and confirm the financials. It's also a good idea to have the property inspected by a professional to uncover any potential issues that could affect its suitability for the Section 8 program.

If the property passes your due diligence, the next step is to secure financing. As we discussed earlier, there are several options available, from traditional mortgages to alternative financing methods. Be sure to work with a lender who understands the Section 8 program and can guide you through the financing process.

Once your financing is in place, it's time to close the deal. This involves signing a mountain of paperwork, but don't let that intimidate you. Take the time to understand each document you're signing, and don't hesitate to ask questions. Remember, this is a significant investment, and it's essential to ensure everything is in order.

After the closing, the real work begins. You'll need to prepare the property for the Section 8 program, which may involve making repairs or upgrades to meet HUD's Housing Quality Standards. You'll also need to apply to your local PHA to have the property approved for the program.

Once your property is approved, you can start advertising it to Section 8 tenants. This involves working with the PHA to list the property and screening potential tenants to find a good fit. Remember, while the PHA provides the housing voucher, you as the landlord have the final say on who rents your property.

Throughout the acquisition process, it's important to stay organized and focused. There will be challenges and setbacks, but with perseverance and a clear strategy, you can successfully navigate the process and acquire a profitable Section 8 property.

The acquisition process is just the beginning of your journey as a Section 8 investor. It's the first step in building a profitable real estate portfolio that can provide you with steady cash flow and long-term financial freedom.

So, are you ready to take the next step in your Section 8 investing journey? If so, let's continue our journey. The path to wealth and financial freedom awaits.

Building Relationships with HUD and Local Authorities

As we delve deeper into the world of Section 8 investing, one thing becomes increasingly clear: the importance of building strong relationships with HUD and local authorities. These relationships can be a crucial factor in your success as a Section 8 landlord, helping you navigate the program's complexities and maximize your investment's potential.

The U.S. Department of Housing and Urban Development (HUD) oversees the Section 8 program at the federal level, but the program is administered locally by Public Housing Agencies (PHAs). These agencies are your primary point of contact for all things related to Section 8. They handle everything from property inspections to tenant applications to rent payments.

Building a positive relationship with your local PHA can make your life as a Section 8 landlord much easier. PHA staff can provide valuable guidance on the program's rules and regulations, help you navigate the inspection process, and even assist in resolving issues with tenants. They can also keep you informed about changes to the program that could affect your investment.

One way to foster a positive relationship with your PHA is to be proactive and communicative. Attend PHA meetings or workshops, ask questions, and seek their advice. Show that you're committed to providing quality housing and working within the program's guidelines. This can go a long way in establishing you as a reliable and cooperative landlord.

In addition to the PHA, it's also beneficial to build relationships with other local authorities. This could include city or county housing departments, zoning boards, and code enforcement agencies. These entities often have a say in housing matters and can be a valuable resource in understanding local regulations and standards.

Remember, these relationships are not just about getting what you need. They're also about contributing positively to your community. By working cooperatively with local authorities, you're showing that you're not just in it for the money. You're also committed to providing safe, decent housing for those who need it most.

In conclusion, building relationships with HUD and local authorities is an integral part of being a successful Section 8 landlord. These relationships can help you navigate the program more effectively, resolve issues more quickly, and ultimately, make your investment more profitable. So, as you embark on your Section 8 investing journey, don't overlook the importance of these connections. They could be the key to your success.

And with that, we wrap up our exploration of the foundations of Section 8 investing. From understanding the program to financing your property, navigating the acquisition process, and building key relationships, we've laid the groundwork for your journey into this rewarding form of real estate investing. Now, it's time to take the next step. Are you ready? Let's continue our journey. The path to wealth and financial freedom awaits.

Chapter 2

PREPARING YOUR PROPERTY FOR SECTION 8

Renovating with Purpose: What Matters to HUD

As we embark on the second chapter of our journey into Section 8 investing, it's time to roll up our sleeves and get our hands dirty. Literally. We're going to talk about renovating your property with a specific purpose in mind: meeting the standards set by HUD.

You see, not just any property qualifies for the Section 8 program. HUD has established strict Housing Quality Standards (HQS) that every Section 8 property must meet. These standards are designed to ensure that all Section 8 housing is safe, sanitary, and suitable for living. They cover everything from basic safety features to the condition of the property's systems and components.

So, what does this mean for you as an investor? It means that when you're renovating a property for the Section 8 program, you need to think beyond just aesthetics or potential rent. You need to consider what matters to HUD.

One of the first things HUD looks at is the overall condition of the property. They want to see that the property is structurally sound, free of health and safety hazards, and in good repair. This means addressing any major issues like a leaky roof, faulty wiring, or a broken HVAC system before anything else.

HUD also pays close attention to the property's systems, including the plumbing, electrical, and heating systems. These systems must be in good working order and meet local building codes. If your property has older systems, you may need to upgrade them to meet these standards.

Another key area that HUD focuses on is safety. This includes things like working smoke detectors, secure windows and doors, and safe, accessible exits in case of emergency. If your property lacks these features, adding them should be a top priority in your renovation plan.

Beyond these basic requirements, HUD also looks at the property's living space. Each unit must have a suitable living area, kitchen, and bathroom. The property must also have adequate space for sleeping, with at least one bedroom or living/sleeping room for every two people.

When renovating with these standards in mind, it's essential to plan carefully and budget accordingly. Some renovations, like fixing a leaky roof or upgrading an electrical system, can be costly. However, these are non-negotiables for HUD, and skimping on them could cost you your Section 8 approval.

It's also a good idea to work with contractors who are familiar with HUD's standards. They can help ensure that your renovations meet HUD's requirements and can potentially save you time and money by avoiding costly mistakes or rework.

Renovating with purpose means more than just making your property look nice. It's about creating a safe, comfortable home that meets HUD's high standards. By focusing on what matters to HUD, you can increase your chances of passing your Section 8 inspection and securing a steady stream of government-backed rent.

So, are you ready to start renovating with purpose? If so, let's continue our journey. The path to wealth and financial freedom awaits.

High-ROI Repairs and Upgrades

As we continue our journey into preparing your property for Section 8, let's shift our focus to a topic that's close to the heart of every real estate investor: return on investment, or ROI. Specifically, we're going to talk about the types of repairs and upgrades that can give you the highest ROI in the context of Section 8 investing.

Now, it's important to understand that high-ROI repairs and upgrades aren't necessarily the same for Section 8 properties as they are for other types of real estate investments. Remember, your goal is not just to increase the property's value or rent potential, but also to meet HUD's Housing Quality Standards. This means that some repairs or upgrades that might not seem as "sexy" or profitable can actually give you a high ROI by helping you pass your Section 8 inspection and secure a steady stream of government-backed rent.

So, what types of repairs and upgrades should you focus on? Here are a few areas to consider:

1. Safety Improvements: As we discussed earlier, safety is a top priority for HUD. This means that investments in safety improvements, like installing smoke detectors, securing windows and doors, or adding handrails and grab bars, can have a high ROI. Not only can these improvements help you pass your Section 8 inspection, but they can also make your property more attractive to potential tenants.

2. System Upgrades: Upgrading your property's systems, such as the plumbing, electrical, or heating system, can be a significant investment. However, these upgrades can also yield a high ROI by ensuring that your property meets HUD's standards and by reducing the risk of costly repairs or maintenance issues down the line.

3. Energy Efficiency: Energy-efficient upgrades, like installing energy-efficient appliances or improving insulation, can be a win-win for both you and your tenants. These upgrades can help lower your property's utility costs, which can be a selling point for potential tenants (especially if they're responsible for paying utilities). Plus, they can help your property meet HUD's requirement for thermal environment.

4. Cosmetic Improvements: While cosmetic improvements might not be as crucial for passing your Section 8 inspection, they can still yield a high ROI by making your property more appealing to potential tenants. This could include things like a fresh coat of paint, new flooring, or updated fixtures.

5. Accessibility: Making your property more accessible can also yield a high ROI, especially if you're targeting older adults or individuals with disabilities. This could include things like installing ramps, widening doorways, or adding a walk-in shower.

Remember, the key to high-ROI repairs and upgrades is to focus on improvements that will help your property meet HUD's standards and appeal to potential tenants. It's not about spending the most money or making the most dramatic changes. It's about making strategic investments that will pay off in the long run.

So, are you ready to start making high-ROI repairs and upgrades to your property? If so, let's continue our journey. The path to wealth and financial freedom awaits.

Setting Up Your Rental for Easy Maintenance

As we further delve into the preparation of your property for Section 8, let's discuss a crucial aspect that often gets overlooked: setting up your rental for easy maintenance. This is an essential step that can save you time, money, and headaches down the line.

When we talk about easy maintenance, we're referring to making strategic choices in your property setup that reduce the frequency and cost of repairs and upkeep. This can range from the materials you choose for your interiors to the layout of your property, and even the appliances and systems you install.

Let's start with the interior. When choosing materials for your floors, walls, and countertops, consider durability and ease of cleaning. For example, hard surface flooring like tile or laminate can be more durable and easier to maintain than carpet, especially in high-traffic areas. Similarly, choosing a semi-gloss paint for walls can make them easier to clean and more resistant to wear and tear.

In the kitchen and bathroom, consider installing fixtures and appliances that are both durable and easy to repair. For instance, a faucet with a common design will be easier (and cheaper) to fix than a unique, high-end model because replacement parts will be readily available. The same goes for appliances; sometimes, the simpler, the better.

Next, let's talk about the property layout. A well-thought-out layout can make routine maintenance tasks easier and more efficient. For example, having all your major systems (like electrical, plumbing, and HVAC) centrally located or easily accessible can save time and effort during inspections or repairs. Similarly, a landscape design that requires minimal upkeep can save on gardening costs and keep the property looking neat with less effort.

Another aspect to consider is the property's systems. Older systems might have a charming, vintage appeal, but they can also be a maintenance nightmare. Upgrading to newer, more efficient systems can reduce the frequency of breakdowns and the need for repairs. Plus, newer systems often come with better warranties, offering additional peace of mind.

It's also worth considering a preventative maintenance plan. Regularly scheduled check-ups for your property's systems can catch potential issues before they turn into costly repairs. This could include annual HVAC inspections, regular plumbing checks, and routine pest control.

Lastly, don't forget about the exterior of your property. Choosing durable, low-maintenance materials for your siding, roof, and outdoor spaces can save on repair costs and keep your property looking its best with minimal effort.

Setting up your rental for easy maintenance is all about thinking ahead and making smart, strategic choices. It might require a bit more effort and investment upfront, but the time, money, and stress it can save you in the long run make it well worth it.

So, are you ready to start setting up your rental for easy maintenance? If so, let's continue our journey. The path to wealth and financial freedom awaits.

The Screening Process: Choosing the Right Section 8 Tenants

Now that we've tackled the physical aspects of preparing your property for Section 8, let's shift our focus to the human element: choosing the right tenants. This is a critical step in your journey as a Section 8 landlord, as the right tenants can make your experience smooth and profitable, while the wrong ones can lead to endless headaches and potential financial loss.

The screening process for Section 8 tenants is similar in many ways to the process for any other rental. However, there are some unique aspects to consider due to the nature of the program. Let's delve into the process and discuss some best practices for choosing the right Section 8 tenants.

First, it's important to understand that while the local Public Housing Agency (PHA) pre-screens tenants for eligibility for the Section 8 program, it's ultimately up to you as the landlord to screen potential tenants for suitability for your property. The PHA's screening process focuses on factors like income, family size, and legal status, but it doesn't necessarily consider things like rental history, creditworthiness, or personal habits that could impact the property.

This is where your screening process comes in. As with any rental, you'll want to start by verifying the potential tenant's income and employment. While Section 8 tenants have their rent subsidized by the government, they are typically required to contribute a portion of their income towards rent. It's important to verify that they can afford their portion.

Next, consider running a credit check. While a low credit score is not uncommon among Section 8 tenants, a history of evictions or unpaid rent should raise a red flag. Remember, a tenant's past behavior is often the best predictor of their future behavior.

One of the most valuable parts of the screening process is checking references. This includes previous landlords and personal references. When speaking with previous landlords, ask about the tenant's payment history, their care for the property, and their overall behavior. Were they respectful and responsible? Did they cause any major issues?

In addition to these standard screening practices, there are a few other factors to consider when screening Section 8 tenants. One is the tenant's voucher size. The voucher size, which is determined by the PHA, dictates the size of the property that the tenant is eligible to rent. Make sure that your property is a suitable match for the tenant's voucher size.

Another factor to consider is the tenant's need for accommodations. Some Section 8 tenants may have disabilities that require certain accommodations, like wheelchair accessibility or visual alarms. Be sure to discuss any such needs with potential tenants to ensure that your property is a good fit.

Finally, trust your instincts. As a landlord, you'll be interacting with your tenants regularly, and it's important to have a good working relationship with them. If something doesn't feel right during the screening process, it may be worth considering other applicants.

Choosing the right Section 8 tenants is a critical step in your journey as a Section 8 landlord. By conducting a thorough screening process, you can increase your chances of finding tenants who will respect your property, pay their rent on time, and contribute to a positive living environment.

So, are you ready to start screening potential tenants for your Section 8 property? If so, let's continue our journey. The path to wealth and financial freedom awaits.

Passing Inspections with Ease

Let's now turn our attention to a crucial step in the Section 8 process: passing inspections. HUD's Housing Quality Standards are strict, and your property must pass an inspection before it can be rented to Section 8 tenants. But don't let this intimidate you. With the right preparation, you can navigate this process with ease.

Firstly, it's important to understand what the inspectors are looking for. They will be checking that your property is safe, clean, and in good repair. They'll examine the condition of the exterior, the plumbing and electrical systems, the heating and cooling systems, and the overall cleanliness and safety of the property. They'll also check for any potential hazards, such as lead-based paint or asbestos.

To pass your inspection with ease, start by addressing any major issues that could be immediate deal-breakers. This might include things like a leaky roof, broken windows, or a faulty heating system. These are things that HUD takes very seriously, and they can cause your property to fail the inspection if not addressed.

Next, turn your attention to smaller, but still important, details. Make sure all electrical outlets and switches are working, that there are no leaks in the plumbing, and that all appliances are in good working order. Check that smoke detectors are installed and working, and that all doors and windows are secure.

Cleanliness is also important. A clean property not only makes a good impression on the inspector, but it also shows that the property is well cared for. So, give your property a thorough cleaning before the inspection. Pay special attention to the kitchen and bathroom, as these areas are often scrutinized.

Finally, remember that preparation is key. Before your inspection, review HUD's Housing Quality Standards and make sure your property meets them. Consider doing a mock inspection with a knowledgeable friend or hire a professional to identify any potential issues.

Passing your Section 8 inspection doesn't have to be a stressful ordeal. With the right preparation and attention to detail, you can navigate this process with ease and get your property ready for your new tenants.

So, are you ready to ace your Section 8 inspection? If so, let's continue our journey. The path to wealth and financial freedom awaits.

Chapter 3

MANAGING SECTION 8 TENANTS LIKE A PRO

Running Your Properties Like a Business

As we embark on the third chapter of our journey into Section 8 investing, it's time to shift our focus from the property itself to the business of being a landlord. Specifically, we're going to talk about running your properties like a business.

You see, being a successful Section 8 landlord is about more than just owning a property and collecting rent. It's about managing your properties effectively, making strategic decisions, and treating your rental activity as a bona fide business. This mindset can make all the difference in your success as a Section 8 landlord.

So, what does it mean to run your properties like a business? Here are a few key principles to keep in mind:

The Ultimate Section 8 Wealth Strategy

1. Have a Plan: Just like any business, successful property management starts with a plan. This should include your goals for the property, your strategies for achieving those goals, and your plans for dealing with potential challenges or setbacks. Your plan should also include a budget, outlining your expected income and expenses.

2. Stay Organized: Good organization is crucial in property management. This means keeping track of all your paperwork, from lease agreements to maintenance records, and staying on top of your financials. Consider using property management software to help keep everything in order.

3. Be Professional: As a landlord, you're not just a property owner; you're also a service provider. This means you need to maintain a professional demeanor in all your interactions with your tenants. Be responsive to their needs, communicate clearly and respectfully, and always uphold your end of the lease agreement.

4. Know the Law: Being a landlord comes with legal responsibilities. Make sure you're familiar with all the laws and regulations that apply to rental properties in your area, including fair housing laws, safety regulations, and the specific rules of the Section 8 program.

5. Continually Learn and Improve: The most successful business owners are those who are always looking for ways to learn and improve. Stay up-to-date on the latest trends and best practices in property management, seek out educational opportunities, and be open to feedback from your tenants and peers.

6. Think Long-Term: Lastly, remember that being a landlord is a long-term endeavor. Don't be swayed by short-term challenges or setbacks. Stay focused on your long-term goals and be patient. The rewards of being a Section 8 landlord can be substantial, but they often take time to realize.

Running your properties like a business is a key aspect of being a successful Section 8 landlord. By adopting a business mindset and following these principles, you can manage your properties effectively, maximize your income, and create a positive living environment for your tenants.

So, are you ready to start running your properties like a business? If so, let's continue our journey. The path to wealth and financial freedom awaits.

Mastering Tenant Relations

As we continue our exploration of managing Section 8 tenants, let's delve into a topic that's at the heart of being a successful landlord: mastering tenant relations. This is a critical aspect of property management that can make or break your experience as a landlord.

Tenant relations is all about building positive, respectful relationships with your tenants. When done right, it can lead to long-term tenancies, fewer vacancies, and less stress for you as a landlord. But it's not always easy. It requires patience, communication, and a commitment to fair and respectful treatment.

Let's start with communication. Clear, timely communication is the cornerstone of good tenant relations. This means keeping your tenants informed about any changes or issues that might affect them, responding promptly to their queries or concerns, and being available when they need you. But it's not just about being responsive; it's also about being proactive. Regular check-ins with your tenants can help you stay ahead of potential problems and show your tenants that you care about their well-being.

Next, let's talk about respect. As a landlord, it's important to treat your tenants with respect and dignity. This means respecting their privacy, listening to their concerns, and addressing any issues in a fair and timely manner. It also means being respectful of their time. For example, if you need to schedule a maintenance visit or inspection, give your tenants plenty of notice and try to schedule it at a time that's convenient for them.

Fair treatment is another key aspect of tenant relations. This means treating all your tenants equally, regardless of their background or circumstances. It also means following all fair housing laws and not discriminating against any tenant or potential tenant. Remember, fair treatment is not just the right thing to do; it's also the law.

Conflict resolution is another important skill in tenant relations. Disputes or disagreements can arise in any landlord-tenant relationship, but how you handle them can make all the difference. When conflicts arise, try to resolve them in a calm, respectful manner. Listen to your tenant's side of the story, try to understand their perspective, and work together to find a solution. If you can't resolve a conflict directly, consider seeking mediation or legal advice.

Finally, remember that good tenant relations is about building relationships. Get to know your tenants as individuals. Show interest in their lives and concerns. Celebrate their successes and offer support during challenging times. Building a personal connection with your tenants can foster a sense of community and make your tenants feel valued and respected.

Mastering tenant relations is a critical aspect of being a successful Section 8 landlord. It requires patience, communication, respect, fair treatment, and a commitment to building relationships. But the rewards - long-term tenancies, fewer vacancies, and a positive, respectful relationship with your tenants - are well worth the effort.

So, are you ready to start mastering tenant relations? If so, let's continue our journey. The path to wealth and financial freedom awaits.

Avoiding the "Tenant from Hell"

As we venture further into the realm of managing Section 8 tenants, we must address a fear that lurks in the minds of many landlords: the dreaded "tenant from hell." We've all heard the horror stories of tenants who cause endless problems, from property damage to late payments, constant complaints, or even legal issues. However, with careful planning and proactive management, you can significantly reduce the chances of encountering such a tenant.

The first line of defense against problematic tenants is a thorough screening process, which we've discussed in the previous chapter. By verifying income, checking credit, contacting references, and meeting potential tenants in person, you can weed out many potential problems before they even start. Remember, the goal is not just to fill vacancies, but to find tenants who will respect your property and abide by the terms of the lease.

In addition to a thorough screening process, clear and comprehensive lease agreements are crucial. A well-written lease sets clear expectations for both parties and provides a legal framework for resolving any disputes that may arise. Be sure to include all necessary terms, such as rent amount and due date, lease duration, security deposit details, maintenance responsibilities, and policies on pets, noise, and other potential issues.

Once a tenant has moved in, proactive management can help prevent small issues from becoming major problems. Regular property inspections can help you catch and address maintenance issues early, before they turn into costly repairs or cause damage to the property. Open lines of communication can help you stay informed about any problems or concerns your tenants may have, allowing you to address them promptly.

Even with the best screening and management practices, you may still encounter challenges with tenants from time to time. In such cases, it's important to handle issues promptly and professionally. If a tenant is consistently late with rent, for example, don't let the problem slide. Address it directly, and if necessary, take legal action to protect your interests.

If you do end up with a problematic tenant, it's important to know your rights and responsibilities as a landlord. Familiarize yourself with the eviction process in your area, and don't hesitate to seek legal advice if necessary. While eviction should always be a last resort, it's an important tool for landlords dealing with serious tenant issues.

Lastly, remember that not all tenant problems are the result of bad behavior. Sometimes, tenants fall on hard times due to job loss, health issues, or other unforeseen circumstances. In such cases, compassion and flexibility can go a long way. If a normally reliable tenant is suddenly struggling to pay rent, for example, you might consider working out a temporary payment plan rather than jumping straight to eviction.

While the "tenant from hell" is a fear for many landlords, such situations are not the norm and can often be avoided with careful screening, proactive management, and clear communication. And even when problems do arise, they can be handled effectively with a combination of firmness, fairness, and, when appropriate, flexibility.

So, are you ready to tackle tenant issues like a pro and avoid the dreaded "tenant from hell"? If so, let's continue our journey. The path to wealth and financial freedom awaits.

Streamlining Rent Collection

Now that we've discussed how to avoid problematic tenants, let's shift our focus to a more positive aspect of property management: collecting rent. After all, rent is the lifeblood of your real estate business, and streamlining the collection process can save you time, reduce stress, and improve your cash flow.

One of the benefits of Section 8 is that a significant portion of the rent is paid directly by the housing authority, providing a reliable source of income each month. However, tenants are typically responsible for a portion of the rent, and collecting this can sometimes be a challenge.

So, how can you streamline rent collection? Here are a few strategies:

1. Make it Easy: The easier you make it for tenants to pay rent, the more likely they are to do so on time. Consider offering multiple payment options, such as online payments, bank transfers, or even direct debit arrangements. The convenience of online payments can be especially appealing to younger tenants.

2. Be Clear About Expectations: Make sure your tenants understand exactly how much they owe each month, when it's due, and what the consequences are for late payments. This should be clearly outlined in the lease agreement, but it's also worth reminding tenants verbally when they move in.

3. Automate Where Possible: Automation can be a game-changer for rent collection. Many property management software platforms offer automated rent collection features, which can save you time and reduce the risk of human error. Automated reminders can also be helpful for ensuring tenants pay on time.

4. Regularly Review Your Process: Even with a good system in place, it's important to regularly review your rent collection process and look for areas of improvement. Are there any common issues or

complaints from tenants? Are there ways you could make the process even more efficient or user-friendly?

5. Be Firm but Fair: While it's important to be understanding if a tenant is genuinely struggling, it's also crucial to enforce your rent collection policies consistently. If a tenant is regularly late with rent, you may need to take further action, such as charging a late fee or ultimately, starting eviction proceedings.

6. Build Good Relationships: Finally, remember that good tenant relationships can make all aspects of property management, including rent collection, smoother. Tenants who feel valued and respected are more likely to take their rental obligations seriously.

Streamlining rent collection is a key aspect of effective property management. By making it easy for tenants to pay, setting clear expectations, automating where possible, and building good relationships, you can ensure a steady flow of income from your properties and reduce the stress and hassle of chasing late payments.

So, are you ready to streamline your rent collection process? If so, let's continue our journey. The path to wealth and financial freedom awaits.

Dealing with Evictions and Legal Issues

As we delve deeper into the realm of managing Section 8 tenants, we inevitably arrive at a topic that no landlord wants to face, but must be prepared for: evictions and legal issues. While we all hope to avoid these situations, understanding how to handle them is crucial to protecting your investment and maintaining a successful rental business.

Evictions are a last resort, but sometimes they are necessary. Whether it's due to non-payment of rent, violation of lease terms, or illegal activity, there may come a time when you need to ask a tenant to leave. The key to handling evictions effectively is to follow the law to the letter. This means providing proper notice, following the correct legal procedures, and treating the tenant fairly throughout the process.

When it comes to legal issues, prevention is often the best strategy. This starts with a solid lease agreement that clearly outlines the rights and responsibilities of both parties. It's also important to stay up-to-date with local and federal housing laws, including fair housing regulations and the specific rules of the Section 8 program. Regular property inspections can also help you catch and address potential issues before they escalate.

If you do find yourself facing a legal issue, don't panic. Take the time to understand the situation and seek legal advice if necessary. Remember, it's better to spend a little money on a lawyer upfront than to risk costly legal problems down the line.

Another key aspect of dealing with legal issues is documentation. Keep detailed records of all interactions with your tenants, as well as any maintenance or repairs on the property. This can provide crucial evidence if a dispute arises.

Finally, remember that evictions and legal issues are often a sign of a deeper problem. If you're constantly dealing with these issues, it may be time to reevaluate your tenant screening process, lease agreements, or property management practices.

While evictions and legal issues are a part of being a landlord, they don't have to be a constant headache. By understanding the law, being proactive, and treating your tenants fairly, you can navigate these challenges effectively and protect your investment.

So, are you ready to tackle evictions and legal issues like a pro? If so, let's continue our journey. The path to wealth and financial freedom awaits.

Chapter 4

SCALING YOUR SECTION 8 EMPIRE

When and How to Expand Your Portfolio

As we turn the page on tenant management, it's time to look towards the future and the exciting prospect of scaling your Section 8 empire. The decision to expand your portfolio is a significant step in your real estate investing journey, one that requires careful planning, strategic thinking, and a keen understanding of the market.

So, when is the right time to expand your portfolio? There's no one-size-fits-all answer to this question, as it depends on a variety of factors. These include your financial situation, the performance of your existing properties, your comfort level with managing more properties, and the state of the real estate market.

However, a good rule of thumb is to consider expanding when your current properties are performing well and you feel confident in your ability to manage additional properties. This means you're consistently receiving rent, your properties are well-maintained, and you have a good relationship with your tenants. It's also important to ensure you have the necessary financial resources to invest in more properties without overextending yourself.

Once you've decided that it's time to expand, the question becomes how to do so effectively. Here are a few strategies to consider:

1. Leverage Your Equity: If your existing properties have appreciated in value, you may be able to leverage the equity in those properties to finance new purchases. This can be a cost-effective way to grow your portfolio, but it's important to do so responsibly to avoid over-leveraging.

2. Focus on Cash Flow Positive Properties: When selecting new properties to add to your portfolio, focus on those that are likely to generate positive cash flow. This means the rental income should cover all expenses, including mortgage payments, property taxes, insurance, and maintenance, with money left over for profit.

3. Diversify Your Portfolio: Consider investing in different types of properties and in different areas. This can help spread risk and increase your chances of success. For example, if you currently own single-family homes, you might consider adding a multi-unit property or a property in a different neighborhood or city.

4. Build a Strong Team: As you expand your portfolio, you'll likely need to rely more on others. This could include property managers,

real estate agents, contractors, and legal or financial advisors. Building a strong team can help you manage your growing portfolio more effectively and free up your time to focus on strategic decision-making.

5. Continually Educate Yourself: The real estate market is constantly evolving, and successful investors are those who stay informed. Make a commitment to continual learning, whether that's through reading, attending seminars, networking with other investors, or seeking professional advice.

Expanding your Section 8 portfolio is an exciting step, but one that should be taken with careful planning and consideration. By leveraging your equity, focusing on cash flow positive properties, diversifying your portfolio, building a strong team, and continually educating yourself, you can scale your empire and build long-term wealth.

So, are you ready to take the leap and start expanding your Section 8 portfolio? If so, let's continue our journey. The path to wealth and financial freedom awaits.

Multi-Unit Properties: The Pros and Cons

As we venture further into the exciting world of scaling your Section 8 empire, let's delve into the topic of multi-unit properties. Investing in multi-unit properties, such as duplexes, triplexes, or apartment buildings, can be a game-changer for your real estate portfolio. However, like all investment strategies, it comes with its own set of pros and cons.

Let's start with the pros. One of the biggest advantages of multi-unit properties is the potential for increased cash flow. With multiple units under one roof, you can generate multiple streams of rental income. This not only boosts your overall income but also provides a buffer if one or more units are vacant.

Another advantage is efficiency. With multi-unit properties, you can manage multiple rental units at the same location. This can save you time and money on property management, maintenance, and repairs. For example, if you need to replace the roof or repaint the exterior, you can do it for multiple units at once.

Multi-unit properties can also offer benefits in terms of financing. Lenders often view these properties as lower risk because the multiple rental incomes can more easily cover the mortgage payments. This can make it easier to secure financing and potentially get better loan terms.

Now, let's talk about the cons. One potential downside is that multi-unit properties often come with higher purchase prices and maintenance costs. This means you'll need more capital upfront, and you may face higher ongoing expenses.

Another challenge is tenant management. With more units comes more tenants, which can mean more potential issues to deal with. This can be especially challenging if you're managing the properties yourself.

Finally, multi-unit properties can be harder to sell than single-family homes. There's a smaller pool of potential buyers, as these properties are typically purchased by investors rather than homebuyers. This can make it harder to sell the property if you need to liquidate your investment.

Investing in multi-unit properties can be a powerful strategy for scaling your Section 8 empire, but it's not without its challenges. It's important to carefully consider the pros and cons, and to do your due diligence before making a purchase. Consider factors like the location, condition of the property, potential rental income, and your ability to manage multiple tenants.

Remember, real estate investing is not a one-size-fits-all game. What works for one investor may not work for another. The key is to find the strategies that align with your goals, resources, and risk tolerance.

So, are you ready to consider adding multi-unit properties to your portfolio? If so, let's continue our journey. The path to wealth and financial freedom awaits.

Funding Your Growth

As we continue our journey into scaling your Section 8 empire, we must address a critical component of growth: funding. Expanding your real estate portfolio requires capital, and understanding how to secure that capital is key to your success.

Let's start with the most traditional route: bank loans. Banks and credit unions offer a variety of loan products for real estate investors, from conventional mortgages to investment property loans. The key to securing a bank loan is having a strong credit score, a stable income, and a solid business plan for your investment property.

However, keep in mind that banks typically require a down payment of 20% or more for investment properties.

Another option is government-backed loans, such as FHA or VA loans. These loans often have lower down payment requirements and more flexible credit criteria, making them a good option for some investors. However, they typically require that you live in one of the units of the property, so they may not be suitable for all investment scenarios.

Private money lenders are another potential source of funding. These are individuals or groups who lend money for real estate investments in exchange for a return on their investment. Private money loans can be more flexible and faster to secure than bank loans, but they also tend to have higher interest rates.

A more creative funding strategy is seller financing. In this scenario, the seller of the property acts as the lender, allowing you to make payments directly to them over time. This can be a good option if you're unable to secure traditional financing, but it requires finding a seller who's willing and able to offer this type of arrangement.

Finally, let's not forget about leveraging your existing assets. If you have equity in your current properties, you may be able to use that equity to fund new purchases. This can be done through a home equity loan, a home equity line of credit, or a cash-out refinance.

While we're on the topic of funding, it's important to mention the role of cash flow in your growth strategy. Positive cash flow from your current properties can be reinvested into new properties, fueling your growth without the need for additional debt. This is why focusing on cash flow positive properties is so crucial in real estate investing.

Funding your growth requires a mix of strategies, from traditional bank loans to creative financing options. The key is to understand your options, assess your financial situation, and choose the strategies that align with your goals and risk tolerance.

So, are you ready to secure the funding you need to scale your Section 8 empire? If so, let's continue our journey. The path to wealth and financial freedom awaits.

Building a Team of Experts

As we continue to navigate the path of scaling your Section 8 empire, we arrive at an important junction: building a team of experts. As your real estate portfolio grows, so too will the demands on your time and expertise. Building a team of professionals can help you manage these demands and ensure the smooth operation of your investments.

Let's start with arguably the most important team member: a property manager. A good property manager can handle the day-to-day operations of your properties, from tenant screening to rent collection to maintenance and repairs. This not only frees up your time but also provides peace of mind knowing that your properties are in good hands. Look for a property manager with experience in Section 8 housing, as they'll be familiar with the unique requirements of this program.

Next up is a real estate agent. While you may have found your first few properties on your own, a knowledgeable real estate agent can be invaluable as you expand your portfolio. They can help you find investment opportunities, negotiate deals, and navigate the closing process. Look for an agent who specializes in investment properties and has a good understanding of the local market.

A real estate attorney is another crucial team member. They can help you navigate the legal aspects of real estate investing, from drafting lease agreements to handling evictions to ensuring compliance with housing laws. While you may not need an attorney on retainer, it's good to have one you can turn to when legal questions arise.

A certified public accountant (CPA) can help you manage the financial aspects of your real estate business. This can include everything from bookkeeping to tax planning to financial analysis. A CPA who specializes in real estate can help you maximize your profits and minimize your tax liability.

Finally, don't forget about the various contractors and service providers you'll need to maintain your properties. This can include plumbers, electricians, landscapers, and more. Having a reliable team of contractors can save you time and headaches when maintenance issues arise.

Building a team of experts isn't just about outsourcing tasks, though. It's about creating a network of professionals who can provide advice, support, and specialized expertise. It's about freeing up your time so you can focus on what you do best: finding and acquiring profitable investment properties.

Remember, real estate is a team sport. The most successful investors are those who know how to leverage the skills and expertise of others. So, don't be afraid to seek help and build relationships. Your team is one of your most valuable assets.

Building a team of experts is a crucial step in scaling your Section 8 empire. By surrounding yourself with knowledgeable professionals, you can ensure the smooth operation of your business, free up your time, and set yourself up for long-term success.

So, are you ready to start building your dream team? If so, let's continue our journey. The path to wealth and financial freedom awaits.

Diversifying Your Real Estate Holdings

As we continue our journey into scaling your Section 8 empire, it's time to discuss an important strategy that can significantly impact your long-term success: diversifying your real estate holdings. Diversification is a key principle in investing, and real estate is no exception. By spreading your investments across different types of properties and markets, you can reduce risk and increase your potential for stable, long-term returns.

When we talk about diversification in real estate, we're referring to two main aspects: property type and location. Let's start with property type. If you've primarily invested in single-family homes, consider exploring other types of properties. Multi-family properties, commercial properties, and even land can offer unique benefits and challenges. Each property type has its own market dynamics, and diversifying across different types can provide a buffer against fluctuations in any one market.

Multi-family properties, for example, can offer higher cash flow and more efficient management compared to single-family homes. Commercial properties, on the other hand, often come with longer lease terms and can be less management-intensive, although they can also require a higher level of expertise and capital.

Next, let's talk about location. If all your properties are in the same neighborhood or city, you're exposed to local market risks. Economic downturns, changes in local laws, or natural disasters can all impact your investments. By diversifying geographically, you can spread this risk. Consider investing in different neighborhoods, cities, or even states. Each market has its own economic drivers, and what affects one may not affect another.

Of course, diversifying geographically comes with its own challenges. Investing in a market you're not familiar with requires careful research and potentially building a new team of local experts. It's also important to consider the logistics of managing properties from a distance.

Diversification is not just about reducing risk, though. It's also about taking advantage of opportunities. Different types of properties and markets can offer different opportunities for profit. By diversifying, you can take advantage of these opportunities as they arise.

Diversifying your real estate holdings is a powerful strategy for scaling your Section 8 empire. By investing in different types of properties and in different markets, you can reduce risk, take advantage of opportunities, and set yourself up for long-term success.

However, remember that diversification is not a substitute for due diligence. Regardless of the type or location of the property, thorough research and analysis are crucial. Always make sure the numbers work and that the investment aligns with your goals and risk tolerance.

So, are you ready to start diversifying your real estate holdings? If so, let's continue our journey. The path to wealth and financial freedom awaits.

Chapter 5

ADVANCED PROPERTY MANAGEMENT TECHNIQUES

Effective Cost Management

As we delve into the world of advanced property management techniques, one of the most critical aspects we need to discuss is effective cost management. In the realm of real estate investing, especially when dealing with Section 8 properties, managing your costs effectively can be the difference between a profitable investment and a financial sinkhole.

Cost management in property management is all about understanding and controlling the expenses associated with owning and operating a rental property. These costs can range from mortgage payments and property taxes to maintenance and repairs, insurance, and property management fees.

One of the first steps in effective cost management is budgeting. Creating a detailed budget for each property can help you anticipate costs, track expenses, and identify areas where you can reduce spending. Your budget should include all fixed costs, like mortgage payments and property taxes, as well as variable costs like repairs and maintenance.

Another key aspect of cost management is preventative maintenance. Regularly inspecting your properties and addressing minor issues before they become major problems can save you significant money in the long run. This could involve regular tasks like cleaning gutters, servicing HVAC systems, and checking for leaks or pest infestations.

Negotiating with vendors and service providers can also help manage costs. Whether it's your property management company, insurance provider, or contractors, don't be afraid to negotiate rates or seek out more affordable options. Just remember, while cost is important, it's also crucial to ensure you're receiving quality service.

Energy efficiency is another area where you can manage costs. Energy-efficient appliances and systems may have a higher upfront cost, but they can save you money over time through lower utility bills. Plus, they can be a selling point for potential tenants.

Finally, don't overlook the potential tax deductions available to real estate investors. Expenses like mortgage interest, property taxes, insurance, maintenance and repairs, and depreciation can all be deducted from your taxable income, reducing your tax liability.

Consult with a tax professional to ensure you're taking advantage of all the deductions available to you.

Effective cost management is a crucial part of advanced property management. By budgeting carefully, maintaining your properties, negotiating with vendors, improving energy efficiency, and maximizing tax deductions, you can control costs and maximize the profitability of your Section 8 properties.

So, are you ready to take control of your property management costs? If so, let's continue our journey. The path to wealth and financial freedom awaits.

Staying Ahead of Inspections

As we continue to delve into advanced property management techniques, let's turn our attention to a critical aspect of managing Section 8 properties: staying ahead of inspections. Regular inspections by the Housing Authority are a part of the Section 8 program, and passing these inspections is crucial to maintaining your status as a Section 8 landlord.

Staying ahead of inspections begins with understanding the inspection process and the standards your property must meet. The Housing Authority uses the Housing Quality Standards (HQS) to evaluate Section 8 properties. These standards cover everything from basic safety features, like working smoke detectors and secure windows and doors, to more specific requirements, like adequate heating and plumbing systems.

Once you understand the standards, the next step is regular self-inspections. Don't wait for the Housing Authority to find problems. Conduct your own inspections regularly and address any issues promptly. This proactive approach can save you time and stress when the official inspection rolls around.

When conducting self-inspections, pay particular attention to common problem areas. These can include safety hazards, like broken windows or railings; plumbing and electrical issues; and problems with heating and cooling systems. Also, check for any potential violations of health codes, like pest infestations or mold.

Another key to staying ahead of inspections is maintaining good relationships with your tenants. Encourage them to report any problems promptly and respond to their concerns quickly. This not only helps you catch and fix problems early but also builds trust with your tenants, which can lead to longer tenancies and fewer vacancies.

If an issue is identified during an official inspection, address it as quickly as possible. The Housing Authority will typically give you a timeframe for making the repairs. Meeting or beating that timeframe shows that you're committed to maintaining your property and meeting your obligations as a Section 8 landlord.

Finally, keep detailed records of all maintenance and repairs. This can provide valuable documentation during inspections or if any disputes arise. It also helps you track your maintenance costs and plan for future expenses.

Staying ahead of inspections is a crucial part of managing Section 8 properties. By understanding the standards, conducting regular self-inspections, maintaining good relationships with tenants, addressing issues promptly, and keeping detailed records, you can navigate the inspection process smoothly and keep your properties in top shape.

So, are you ready to stay ahead of inspections and ensure your properties meet the highest standards? If so, let's continue our journey. The path to wealth and financial freedom awaits.

Tenant Retention Strategies

As we delve further into advanced property management techniques, it's time to discuss a critical aspect of success: tenant retention. Keeping good tenants in your properties is far more cost-effective than constantly finding new ones. Plus, long-term tenants can provide a stable income stream, reduce wear and tear on your property, and contribute to a positive community atmosphere.

One of the most effective tenant retention strategies is to provide excellent customer service. This starts with being responsive and attentive to your tenants' needs. Whether it's a maintenance request or a question about their lease, respond promptly and professionally. Show your tenants that you value them and are committed to providing a high-quality living experience.

Regular maintenance and upgrades can also contribute to tenant retention. No one wants to live in a property that's falling into disrepair. Regularly inspect your properties and address maintenance issues promptly. Also, consider periodic upgrades to keep your properties modern and appealing. This could be as simple as a fresh coat of paint or as significant as a kitchen remodel.

Another strategy is to foster a sense of community among your tenants. This can be particularly effective in multi-family properties. Organize community events, create shared spaces where tenants can interact, and encourage a sense of neighborliness. When tenants feel connected to their community, they're more likely to stay.

Fair and transparent communication is also crucial. Be clear about your policies and expectations, and be fair and consistent in enforcing them. Also, keep tenants informed about any changes or issues that may affect them. This can build trust and show your tenants that you respect them and value their tenancy.

Finally, consider offering incentives for lease renewals. This could be a rent discount, a property upgrade, or even a simple thank you note. Small gestures can go a long way in showing your tenants that you appreciate them.

Tenant retention should be a key part of your property management strategy. By providing excellent customer service, maintaining and upgrading your properties, fostering a sense of community, communicating fairly and transparently, and offering renewal incentives, you can keep your properties filled with happy, long-term tenants.

So, are you ready to implement these tenant retention strategies and enjoy the benefits of long-term tenancies? If so, let's continue our journey. The path to wealth and financial freedom awaits.

Leveraging Technology in Property Management

As we continue to explore advanced property management techniques, it's time to address a critical component that can significantly streamline your operations: technology. In today's digital age, leveraging technology in property management can save you time, reduce errors, and enhance your tenants' experience.

One of the most impactful ways to leverage technology is through property management software. These platforms can automate many of the tasks involved in managing rental properties, from tracking rent payments to scheduling maintenance requests. They can also provide valuable insights into your properties' performance, helping you make data-driven decisions.

Online rent collection is another technological tool that can simplify your operations. It's convenient for both you and your tenants, eliminating the need for paper checks and trips to the bank. Plus, with automatic payment options, you can reduce late or missed payments.

Digital communication tools can also enhance your property management. Email, text messaging, and even social media can provide efficient ways to communicate with your tenants. Whether you're sending rent reminders, notifying tenants about maintenance work, or just checking in, digital communication can make the process quicker and easier.

Virtual tours and online listings are another way to leverage technology. These tools can help you attract prospective tenants and fill vacancies faster. Virtual tours allow potential tenants to explore your properties from the comfort of their own homes, which can be particularly valuable in today's increasingly online world.

Technology can also assist with record keeping. Digital storage solutions can help you keep track of important documents, like lease agreements, maintenance records, and financial reports. This not only saves physical space but also makes it easier to find and access the information you need.

Finally, smart home technology can be a valuable addition to your properties. Features like smart thermostats, security systems, and keyless entry can attract tenants and even allow you to command higher rents. Plus, some smart home features can help you monitor and manage your properties more efficiently.

However, while technology can offer many benefits, it's important to use it wisely. Be mindful of privacy concerns, particularly when using smart home technology or digital communication tools. Also, remember that technology is a tool to enhance your property management, not replace the personal touch that can make a real difference in tenant satisfaction.

Leveraging technology in property management can streamline your operations, enhance your tenants' experience, and help you manage your properties more effectively. From property management software to smart home features, there are many ways to use technology to your advantage.

So, are you ready to embrace technology and take your property management to the next level? If so, let's continue our journey. The path to wealth and financial freedom awaits.

Dealing with Unexpected Challenges

In the world of property management, unexpected challenges are part of the game. From sudden maintenance issues to changes in housing regulations, being prepared to handle these challenges is crucial to your success.

One of the most common unexpected challenges is maintenance emergencies. Whether it's a burst pipe, a broken furnace in the middle of winter, or a gas leak, these issues need to be addressed immediately to keep your tenants safe and your property intact. Having a reliable network of contractors who can respond quickly is essential. Also, setting aside a contingency fund for these unexpected costs can help you handle them without disrupting your cash flow.

Changes in housing laws and regulations can also present challenges. These can range from new safety requirements to changes in eviction laws. Staying informed about the latest laws and regulations in your area is crucial. Joining local landlord associations or real estate investment groups can be a great way to stay up to date.

Tenant issues are another common challenge. From late rent payments to lease violations to disputes between tenants, these issues can be time-consuming and stressful. Having clear policies and procedures in place can help you handle these situations fairly and consistently. It's also important to communicate clearly and professionally with your tenants, and to document all interactions in case disputes escalate.

Finally, market fluctuations can present unexpected challenges. Changes in the local economy can affect rental demand and prices. Regularly reviewing market trends and adjusting your strategies accordingly can help you navigate these fluctuations. Remember, real estate is a long-term investment, and short-term market changes are part of the journey.

Dealing with unexpected challenges is a key part of property management. By preparing for emergencies, staying informed about laws and regulations, managing tenant issues effectively, and navigating market fluctuations, you can handle these challenges and keep your properties running smoothly.

So, are you ready to tackle the unexpected and keep your property management game strong? If so, let's continue our journey. The path to wealth and financial freedom awaits.

Chapter 6

THE LEGAL SIDE OF SECTION 8 INVESTING

Understanding Your Legal Responsibilities

As we embark on Chapter 6, we delve into the legal side of Section 8 investing, an area that is just as important as understanding market trends and property management. The first step in navigating the legal landscape is understanding your legal responsibilities as a Section 8 landlord.

Being a Section 8 landlord comes with specific responsibilities, many of which are outlined in the Housing Assistance Payments (HAP) contract you sign with the Housing Authority. This contract stipulates that you must maintain your property according to the Housing Quality Standards (HQS) set by the U.S. Department of Housing and Urban Development (HUD). Regular inspections will be conducted to ensure these standards are met. Failure to comply can result in the termination of your contract and loss of rental income.

In addition to maintaining your property, you are also legally obligated to respect the rights of your tenants. This includes not discriminating against tenants based on race, color, national origin, religion, sex, family status, or disability. It's essential to understand and comply with the Fair Housing Act to avoid legal issues and penalties.

Another critical legal responsibility is honoring the terms of the lease agreement. This agreement should outline the rights and responsibilities of both the landlord and the tenant, including rent amount and payment terms, length of the lease, and rules regarding pets, noise, and other potential issues. Breaking the terms of the lease can lead to legal consequences.

You are also responsible for handling security deposits legally. Each state has laws regarding how security deposits should be handled, including how much can be charged, where the money should be stored, and how and when it should be returned to the tenant. Familiarize yourself with your state's laws to avoid legal pitfalls.

Lastly, in the unfortunate event of needing to evict a tenant, you must follow the legal eviction process. This typically involves giving notice to the tenant, filing an eviction lawsuit, and obtaining a court order. Attempting to evict a tenant without following the legal process, such as by changing the locks or shutting off utilities, can lead to legal trouble.

Understanding your legal responsibilities is a crucial part of being a successful Section 8 landlord. By maintaining your property, respecting tenant rights, honoring lease agreements, handling security deposits correctly, and following the legal eviction process, you can protect yourself legally and provide a safe, fair living environment for your tenants.

So, are you ready to understand and fulfill your legal responsibilities as a Section 8 landlord? If so, let's continue our journey. The path to wealth and financial freedom awaits.

Crafting Bulletproof Leases

As we continue to navigate the legal side of Section 8 investing, let's focus on an essential tool in your landlord toolkit: the lease agreement. A well-crafted lease can protect you legally, set clear expectations for your tenants, and help prevent disputes down the line.

Crafting a bulletproof lease starts with understanding the basic elements that should be included. These typically include the names of the landlord and tenant, the property address, the term of the lease, the amount of rent and when it's due, and the amount of the security deposit.

But a bulletproof lease goes beyond the basics. It should also outline the responsibilities of both parties. This includes who is responsible for utilities, maintenance and repairs, and adhering to community rules. Be as specific as possible to avoid misunderstandings.

One critical area to address in your lease is the Section 8 program rules. Make sure your lease complies with HUD regulations and the terms of your Housing Assistance Payments (HAP) contract. This includes not charging more than the approved rent and not terminating the lease without good cause.

Your lease should also include clauses to protect you legally. This might include a clause stating that the tenant will use the property for residential purposes only, a clause outlining the conditions under which you can enter the property, and a clause stating that the tenant will comply with all applicable laws and regulations.

It's also important to include a clause about lease termination. This should specify the conditions under which the lease can be terminated, the notice required, and the process for eviction. Remember, evictions must comply with state law and the terms of your HAP contract.

Finally, consider including a severability clause. This states that if one part of the lease is found to be invalid, the rest of the lease still stands. This can protect you if a dispute arises and a court finds one clause of your lease to be unenforceable.

Remember, while you can find lease templates online, it's important to customize your lease to fit your property and situation. Laws can also vary by state, so it's a good idea to have a local real estate attorney review your lease to ensure it's legally sound.

A bulletproof lease is a key component of protecting yourself legally as a Section 8 landlord. By including all the necessary elements, outlining responsibilities clearly, complying with Section 8 rules, including protective clauses, and having your lease reviewed by an attorney, you can create a lease that serves as a strong foundation for your landlord-tenant relationships.

So, are you ready to craft a bulletproof lease that protects you and sets clear expectations for your tenants? If so, let's continue our journey. The path to wealth and financial freedom awaits.

Avoiding Legal Pitfalls

As we continue our journey through the legal landscape of Section 8 investing, let's turn our attention to avoiding legal pitfalls. Being aware of potential legal issues and taking steps to prevent them can save you significant time, money, and stress down the line.

One of the most common legal pitfalls is non-compliance with fair housing laws. The Fair Housing Act prohibits discrimination based on race, color, national origin, religion, sex, familial status, or disability. This applies to all aspects of the landlord-tenant relationship, from advertising your property to selecting tenants to setting rent amounts. Violating these laws can result in severe penalties, so it's crucial to understand and comply with them.

Another common pitfall is neglecting property maintenance. As a Section 8 landlord, you're required to maintain your property according to Housing Quality Standards (HQS). Failure to do so can lead to the termination of your Housing Assistance Payments (HAP) contract, loss of rental income, and potential legal action from tenants. Regular inspections and prompt repairs can help you avoid these issues.

Improper handling of security deposits can also lead to legal trouble. Each state has laws regarding how much you can charge for a security deposit, where the funds should be kept, and when and how the deposit should be returned to the tenant. Non-compliance with these laws can result in penalties and damage your relationship with your tenants.

Evicting a tenant improperly is another legal pitfall to avoid. The eviction process is governed by state law and the terms of your HAP contract, and typically involves giving notice to the tenant, filing an eviction lawsuit, and obtaining a court order. Attempting to evict a tenant without following the legal process, such as by changing the locks or shutting off utilities, can lead to legal action against you.

Finally, failing to protect your personal assets can be a major legal pitfall. If a tenant or their guest is injured on your property and you're found to be at fault, you could be held personally liable. Forming a Limited Liability Company (LLC) for your rental properties can provide a layer of protection for your personal assets. Also, having adequate insurance coverage, including liability insurance, can protect you in the event of a lawsuit.

Avoiding legal pitfalls is a crucial part of being a successful Section 8 landlord. By complying with fair housing laws, maintaining your property, handling security deposits correctly, following the legal eviction process, and protecting your personal assets, you can navigate the legal landscape of Section 8 investing with confidence.

So, are you ready to avoid legal pitfalls and protect your real estate investment? If so, let's continue our journey. The path to wealth and financial freedom awaits.

How to Handle Tenant Disputes

As we delve deeper into the legal aspects of Section 8 investing, it's crucial to discuss how to handle tenant disputes. No matter how well you manage your properties, disagreements are inevitable. However, the way you handle these disputes can make a significant difference in maintaining a positive landlord-tenant relationship and avoiding legal complications.

One of the most effective ways to handle tenant disputes is to maintain open and clear communication. Many disagreements arise from misunderstandings or miscommunications. By being accessible and willing to listen, you can often resolve issues before they escalate. Remember, your tenants are your customers, and treating them with respect and understanding can go a long way.

When a dispute arises, take the time to understand the tenant's perspective. Ask for their side of the story and listen without interrupting. This can help defuse tension and show the tenant that you value their input.

Once you understand the issue, review your lease agreement and any relevant laws or regulations. Your lease should be the guiding document for resolving disputes, as it outlines the rights and responsibilities of both parties. If the dispute involves a gray area not covered by the lease, consult local and federal housing laws or seek advice from a real estate attorney.

In some cases, you may need to negotiate a resolution. This could involve compromising on a point of contention or offering something in return for the tenant's cooperation. Remember, it's often more cost-effective to resolve a dispute amicably than to let it escalate to legal action.

If a dispute can't be resolved through communication and negotiation, you may need to consider mediation. A neutral third party can facilitate a conversation between you and the tenant, helping you reach a mutually acceptable resolution. Many local housing authorities and community organizations offer free or low-cost mediation services.

In the rare case that a dispute escalates to a lawsuit, it's crucial to have legal representation. A real estate attorney can guide you through the process and help protect your interests. Also, having comprehensive records of all interactions with your tenant, including the dispute in question, can be invaluable in a legal proceeding.

Handling tenant disputes effectively is a crucial part of being a successful Section 8 landlord. By maintaining open communication, understanding your lease and relevant laws, negotiating when necessary, considering mediation, and seeking legal representation if needed, you can navigate tenant disputes with confidence.

So, are you ready to handle tenant disputes like a pro? If so, let's continue our journey. The path to wealth and financial freedom awaits.

Insurance and Liability Protection

As we round off our exploration of the legal side of Section 8 investing, it's crucial to discuss insurance and liability protection. These are essential components of your risk management strategy, protecting you from financial losses due to property damage, legal claims, and other potential risks.

One of the key types of insurance you'll need as a landlord is property insurance. This covers damage to your property due to events like fire, storms, and vandalism. It's important to ensure your policy covers the full replacement cost of your property, not just its current market value. Also, consider whether you need additional coverage for events not typically covered by standard policies, like floods or earthquakes.

Liability insurance is another must-have. This covers legal costs and potential damages if someone is injured on your property and you're found to be at fault. This could include a tenant, a visitor, or even a contractor working on your property. It's crucial to have enough liability coverage to protect your assets in case of a lawsuit.

Loss of income insurance, also known as rental default insurance, is another valuable coverage to consider. This can cover lost rental income if your property becomes uninhabitable due to a covered event, like a fire or major water damage. While Section 8 landlords have some protection against loss of income due to guaranteed government payments, this insurance can provide additional protection if the property itself is out of commission.

In addition to these insurance coverages, consider forming a Limited Liability Company (LLC) for your rental properties. An LLC can provide a layer of protection for your personal assets in case of a lawsuit. If a claim exceeds your insurance coverage, the LLC's assets would be at risk, not your personal assets. However, forming an LLC involves costs and additional paperwork, so weigh these against the potential benefits.

Lastly, always maintain your property to a high standard. Regular inspections and prompt repairs can prevent many issues that could lead to insurance claims or lawsuits. Plus, a well-maintained property is more likely to attract and retain quality tenants.

Insurance and liability protection are crucial aspects of managing the legal risks of Section 8 investing. By having the right insurance coverages, considering an LLC, and maintaining your property well, you can protect your investment and ensure your journey to financial freedom continues smoothly.

So, are you ready to protect your investment with the right insurance and liability protection? If so, let's continue our journey. The path to wealth and financial freedom awaits.

Chapter 7

HANDLING DIFFICULT TENANTS AND SITUATIONS

Dealing with Non-Paying Tenants

As we venture into Chapter 7, we'll tackle one of the most challenging aspects of being a landlord: handling difficult tenants and situations. Let's start by discussing how to deal with non-paying tenants, a situation that can be particularly stressful and financially draining.

One of the benefits of being a Section 8 landlord is the assurance of a portion of your rent being paid directly by the government. However, tenants are still responsible for paying their portion of the rent, and there may be instances when they fail to do so.

When dealing with non-paying tenants, the first step is to communicate. Reach out to the tenant to understand why the payment is late. It could be a simple oversight, a temporary financial hardship, or a more serious issue. Remember to approach the conversation with empathy and professionalism. Your goal is to understand the situation and work towards a resolution, not to escalate the conflict.

If the tenant is experiencing temporary financial difficulties, consider working out a payment plan. This can help the tenant manage their financial obligations and ensure you receive the owed rent. Make sure to document any agreed-upon payment plan in writing to avoid misunderstandings later.

If the tenant repeatedly fails to pay their portion of the rent or refuses to communicate, you may need to consider more formal steps. This could involve serving a pay or quit notice, which is a formal document that gives the tenant a specific period to pay the overdue rent or vacate the property. The timeframe and requirements for this notice vary by state, so it's important to understand your local laws.

In some cases, you may need to involve the local housing authority. They can provide guidance and may be able to assist in resolving the issue. If the tenant continues to not pay their portion of the rent, the housing authority may terminate their voucher, making them ineligible for Section 8 assistance.

If all else fails, you may need to consider eviction. This is a last resort and involves a legal process that varies by state. It's crucial to follow this process exactly to avoid legal complications. Remember, you cannot evict a tenant without a court order, and you cannot force a tenant out by changing locks or shutting off utilities.

Dealing with non-paying tenants can be challenging, but by communicating effectively, considering payment plans, understanding your legal options, and involving the housing authority when necessary, you can navigate this situation. Remember, prevention is key. Thorough tenant screening and clear communication about rent expectations can help prevent non-payment issues from arising in the first place.

So, are you ready to handle non-paying tenants effectively? If so, let's continue our journey. The path to wealth and financial freedom awaits.

Evicting Problem Tenants

As we continue to explore the challenges of handling difficult tenants and situations, let's discuss one of the most daunting tasks a landlord may face: evicting problem tenants. While it's a situation no landlord wants to find themselves in, understanding the eviction process is crucial for maintaining control over your property and protecting your investment.

Firstly, it's important to understand that eviction is a legal process, and it's essential to follow the law meticulously. This means you cannot resort to "self-help" evictions, such as changing the locks or turning off utilities, to force a tenant out. Such actions can lead to legal repercussions.

The eviction process typically begins with a notice to the tenant. This could be a "pay or quit" notice for non-payment of rent, or a "cure or quit" notice for violations of the lease agreement. The specifics of these notices, including how they must be delivered and the timeframe the tenant has to rectify the situation, vary by state.

If the tenant fails to respond to the notice by either remedying the issue or vacating the property, the next step is to file an eviction lawsuit, also known as an unlawful detainer lawsuit, with your local court. This involves submitting the necessary paperwork and paying a filing fee. The court will then set a date for an eviction hearing.

During the hearing, you'll need to present your case to the judge. This is where your record-keeping comes into play. Documentation of rent payments, copies of any notices you've given the tenant, records of communication, and a copy of the lease agreement can all serve as crucial evidence.

If the judge rules in your favor, they will issue a judgment for possession. This is a court order that allows you to regain possession of your property. In some states, the tenant may have a few days to leave voluntarily after the judgment is issued. If they don't, you can request a writ of possession from the court, which allows the local sheriff to remove the tenant and their belongings.

It's important to note that the eviction process can be complex and time-consuming. It's often advisable to seek legal counsel to ensure you're following the law every step of the way. Also, remember that as a Section 8 landlord, you must also comply with HUD regulations during the eviction process.

While evicting a problem tenant can be a challenging process, understanding the legal steps involved can help you navigate it effectively. By maintaining good records, following the law to the letter, and seeking legal counsel when necessary, you can handle this difficult situation with confidence.

So, are you ready to handle the eviction process like a pro? If so, let's continue our journey. The path to wealth and financial freedom awaits.

Tenant Damage Control

As we delve further into handling difficult tenants and situations, let's tackle the issue of tenant damage control. Property damage can be a significant headache for landlords, leading to unexpected repair costs and potential disputes with tenants. However, with the right strategies, you can minimize damage and handle any issues that arise effectively.

Firstly, prevention is the best form of damage control. Having a comprehensive lease agreement that clearly outlines the tenant's responsibilities regarding property care is crucial. This should include stipulations about what modifications or alterations the tenant can make, their responsibility for minor repairs, and the consequences of causing damage beyond normal wear and tear.

Regular property inspections are another key preventive measure. These allow you to catch and address minor issues before they become major problems. They also send a message to your tenants that you're serious about property maintenance. While conducting these inspections, it's important to respect your tenants' privacy and provide adequate notice, as required by law.

Despite your best preventive efforts, damage may still occur. When it does, it's important to address it promptly and professionally. Assess the damage and determine whether it falls under normal wear and tear, which is typically the landlord's responsibility, or if it's excessive damage caused by the tenant.

If the tenant is responsible for the damage, you should notify them in writing, detailing the nature of the damage, the cost of repairs, and how this will be covered. Typically, you would deduct the cost from the tenant's security deposit. However, if the cost exceeds the deposit, you may need to bill the tenant for the additional amount.

In some cases, you may need to involve your insurance company, especially if the damage is extensive. This is where having a comprehensive landlord insurance policy comes into play. It's also advisable to document the damage thoroughly with photos and written descriptions in case of disputes or for insurance claims.

Handling damage disputes with tenants can be tricky. It's important to remain professional and stick to the facts. If a tenant disputes their responsibility for the damage or the cost of repairs, refer back to your lease agreement and your documentation of the damage. In some cases, you may need to seek legal advice or mediation to resolve the dispute.

While property damage can be a challenging aspect of being a landlord, you can manage it effectively with clear lease agreements, regular property inspections, prompt and professional responses to damage, thorough documentation, and the right insurance coverage. Remember, your goal is not just to protect your property, but also to maintain a positive landlord-tenant relationship.

So, are you ready to handle tenant damage like a pro? If so, let's continue our journey. The path to wealth and financial freedom awaits.

Handling Tenant Complaints and Disputes

As we continue navigating the challenges of dealing with difficult tenants and situations, let's discuss how to handle tenant complaints and disputes. As a landlord, you're bound to encounter complaints, ranging from maintenance issues to disagreements over the lease terms. How you handle these complaints can significantly impact your relationship with your tenants and the overall success of your investment.

Firstly, it's important to maintain an open line of communication with your tenants. Encourage them to bring their concerns to you directly. This not only helps you address issues promptly but also builds trust with your tenants. They need to know that you're approachable and committed to providing a safe and comfortable living environment.

When a complaint arises, respond promptly and professionally. Even if you can't immediately resolve the issue, acknowledging the complaint and assuring the tenant that you're working on it can go a long way in maintaining a positive relationship. Remember, your tenants are your customers, and good customer service is key in any business.

Understanding the nature of the complaint is crucial. Is it a maintenance issue? A dispute over the lease agreement? A problem with another tenant? Each type of complaint requires a different approach. For maintenance issues, have a reliable team of contractors or handymen ready to address problems quickly. For lease disputes, refer back to your lease agreement and consult with a lawyer if necessary.

Sometimes, you may need to mediate disputes between tenants. In such cases, it's important to remain neutral and listen to all parties involved. Encourage open communication and try to facilitate a resolution that respects everyone's rights and maintains a peaceful living environment.

Documenting complaints and your responses is also crucial. This can provide a reference for future interactions with the tenant and can be invaluable in case of legal disputes. Keep a record of all communications, including dates, times, and the nature of the discussions.

If a complaint escalates into a dispute, consider seeking help from a mediator. Many local housing authorities and community organizations offer mediation services. A neutral third party can help facilitate a conversation and guide you and the tenant towards a mutually agreeable resolution.

Handling tenant complaints and disputes is a vital part of being a landlord. By maintaining open communication, responding promptly and professionally, understanding the nature of the complaint, mediating when necessary, and keeping thorough records, you can navigate these challenges effectively. Remember, your goal is to provide a safe and comfortable home for your tenants while protecting your investment.

So, are you ready to handle tenant complaints and disputes like a pro? If so, let's continue our journey. The path to wealth and financial freedom awaits.

Safety Measures for Landlords

As we wrap up our discussion on handling difficult tenants and situations, it's important to touch on the topic of safety measures for landlords. Ensuring your safety, as well as that of your tenants, is paramount in the real estate business.

First and foremost, it's crucial to ensure that your properties are safe and up to code. Regular inspections can help identify potential safety hazards, such as faulty wiring, leaks, or structural issues. Addressing these promptly not only protects your tenants but also helps avoid potential liability issues down the line.

When it comes to interacting with tenants, always maintain professionalism. This includes keeping communication primarily about business matters and avoiding unnecessary personal involvement. This not only helps maintain boundaries but also protects you from potential misunderstandings or disputes.

If you need to visit the property for inspections or maintenance, always give your tenants proper notice as required by law. Not only is this a legal requirement, but it also respects your tenants' privacy and helps maintain a positive landlord-tenant relationship. If possible, try to schedule these visits during daylight hours and let someone know where you're going for added safety.

In the unfortunate event that a dispute with a tenant escalates, it's important to stay calm and professional. Avoid confrontations and seek legal advice if necessary. Remember, it's not just about winning an argument, but about maintaining a safe and respectful business relationship.

Finally, consider investing in a landlord insurance policy that includes liability coverage. This can protect you financially in case of accidents or injuries on your property. While insurance can't prevent incidents, it can provide a financial safety net if something goes wrong.

Safety should always be a top priority for landlords. By ensuring your properties are safe, maintaining professional boundaries, giving proper notice for visits, staying calm during disputes, and having adequate insurance, you can protect yourself and your tenants.

So, are you ready to prioritize safety in your real estate business? If so, let's continue our journey. The path to wealth and financial freedom awaits.

Chapter 8

STRATEGIC PROPERTY MAINTENANCE

Low-Cost, High-Impact Repairs

As we embark on Chapter 8, we delve into the world of strategic property maintenance. One of the keys to successful real estate investing is knowing how to maintain and improve your properties without breaking the bank. Let's start by discussing low-cost, high-impact repairs.

When it comes to property maintenance, not all repairs are created equal. Some repairs can significantly enhance your property's appeal and value without requiring a large investment. These are the types of repairs you want to focus on as a savvy real estate investor.

One of the most cost-effective repairs is a fresh coat of paint. It's amazing how much a clean, fresh paint job can brighten a property and make it more appealing to tenants. Opt for neutral colors that will appeal to a wide range of people and make the space feel larger and brighter.

Another low-cost, high-impact repair is replacing outdated or worn-out fixtures. This could include light fixtures, faucets, door handles, and cabinet hardware. These small details can significantly modernize a property and make it more attractive to potential tenants.

Flooring is another area where a small investment can make a big difference. If your property has worn-out carpet, consider replacing it with laminate or vinyl plank flooring. These materials are relatively inexpensive, durable, and easy to clean, making them a great choice for rental properties.

Upgrading the landscaping is another cost-effective way to improve a property's curb appeal. This doesn't have to involve a complete overhaul. Simple steps like keeping the lawn mowed, planting some colorful flowers, or adding a few shrubs can make a big difference.

Lastly, don't underestimate the impact of a thorough cleaning. A sparkling clean property is much more appealing to potential tenants than one that's grimy or neglected. Hiring a professional cleaning service before showing the property can be a worthwhile investment.

Strategic property maintenance is all about getting the most bang for your buck. By focusing on low-cost, high-impact repairs like fresh paint, fixture replacements, flooring upgrades, simple landscaping, and thorough cleaning, you can significantly enhance your property's appeal without draining your bank account.

So, are you ready to make smart, cost-effective repairs to your properties? If so, let's continue our journey. The path to wealth and financial freedom awaits.

Preventative Maintenance Tips

As we continue our journey through strategic property maintenance, let's turn our attention to preventative maintenance. This proactive approach can help you avoid costly repairs and extend the life of your property's key systems and components.

One of the most important aspects of preventative maintenance is regular inspections. By checking your property regularly, you can spot potential issues before they become major problems. This could include checking for leaks, inspecting the roof, testing smoke and carbon monoxide detectors, and checking the HVAC system.

When it comes to the HVAC system, regular servicing is crucial. Have a professional clean and service the system at least once a year. This can help prevent unexpected breakdowns and keep the system running efficiently, saving you money on energy costs.

Plumbing is another area where preventative maintenance can save you a lot of headaches. Regularly check for leaks, and address any issues promptly. Even a small leak can lead to significant water damage over time. Also, consider having your property's sewer line inspected and cleaned periodically to prevent backups.

Your property's exterior also needs regular maintenance to prevent issues. Keep the gutters clean to prevent water damage, and regularly check the roof for any signs of damage or wear. Also, make sure the property's drainage is good, with water flowing away from the foundation to prevent flooding or structural damage.

Another key aspect of preventative maintenance is keeping up with routine tasks like changing air filters, testing smoke and carbon monoxide detectors, and servicing major appliances. These tasks can help prevent larger issues down the line.

Finally, don't forget about pest control. Regular inspections and preventative treatments can help keep pests at bay and prevent infestations that can cause significant damage.

Preventative maintenance is a crucial part of strategic property maintenance. By regularly inspecting your property, servicing key systems, addressing small issues promptly, and keeping up with routine tasks, you can prevent major issues and save money in the long run.

So, are you ready to take a proactive approach to property maintenance? If so, let's continue our journey. The path to wealth and financial freedom awaits.

Finding Reliable Contractors

As we delve deeper into the realm of strategic property maintenance, let's tackle the topic of finding reliable contractors. Whether it's for a simple repair or a major renovation, having a dependable contractor can make a world of difference in maintaining and improving your property.

The first step in finding a reliable contractor is to do your research. Start by asking for recommendations from other landlords or real estate professionals in your area. They can often provide firsthand accounts of their experiences with local contractors. You can also use online resources like contractor directories and review sites to find contractors and see what others have to say about their work.

Once you have a few potential contractors in mind, it's time to vet them. Check their credentials, including licensing, insurance, and any relevant certifications. You should also ask for references and actually follow up on them. Speaking with past clients can give you a good sense of the contractor's reliability, quality of work, and professionalism.

Getting written estimates from multiple contractors can also be beneficial. This not only gives you an idea of the cost but also allows you to compare what each contractor is offering. Be wary of estimates that seem too good to be true—they often are.

When you're ready to hire a contractor, get everything in writing. This includes the scope of work, the cost, the payment schedule, and any warranties or guarantees. A written contract protects both you and the contractor and helps prevent misunderstandings down the line.

Remember, the cheapest contractor isn't always the best choice. It's worth paying a bit more for a contractor who is reliable, communicates well, and does high-quality work. After all, the goal is to protect and enhance your investment.

Finally, once you've found a reliable contractor, work on building a good relationship with them. Being a good client can help ensure that your projects get prioritized and that you have a go-to contractor for future needs.

Finding a reliable contractor is a crucial part of strategic property maintenance. By doing your research, vetting potential contractors, getting written estimates and contracts, and building strong relationships, you can ensure that your property is in good hands.

So, are you ready to find reliable contractors for your properties? If so, let's continue our journey. The path to wealth and financial freedom awaits.

Budgeting for Repairs and Maintenance

As we continue to explore the realm of strategic property maintenance, let's turn our attention to budgeting for repairs and maintenance. This is a critical aspect of property management that, when handled correctly, can prevent financial surprises and help ensure the longevity of your real estate investment.

One of the first steps in budgeting for repairs and maintenance is to understand the average costs associated with owning a rental property. As a general rule of thumb, you should set aside 1% to 2% of the property's value each year for maintenance. For example, if your property is worth $200,000, you should budget $2,000 to $4,000 per year for maintenance costs.

However, this is just a rough estimate. The actual amount you'll need can vary depending on the age and condition of the property, the quality of its construction, the weather conditions in your area, and other factors. Older properties or those in areas with harsh weather conditions may require a higher maintenance budget.

Another important factor to consider is the difference between repairs and capital improvements. Repairs are necessary to keep the property in good working condition and are typically less expensive. These might include fixing a leaky faucet or patching a hole in the wall. Capital improvements, on the other hand, add value to the property and usually cost more. These might include replacing the roof or installing a new HVAC system.

It's also wise to build a contingency fund into your budget. This is money set aside to cover unexpected expenses. A good rule of thumb is to set aside an additional 10% to 20% of your annual maintenance budget for contingencies.

When budgeting for repairs and maintenance, it's important to keep track of your expenses. This can help you adjust your budget as necessary and provides valuable information for tax purposes. You can use a simple spreadsheet or a property management software to track your maintenance costs.

Budgeting for repairs and maintenance is a key aspect of strategic property maintenance. By understanding the average costs, distinguishing between repairs and capital improvements, building a contingency fund, and tracking your expenses, you can manage your maintenance budget effectively and protect your real estate investment.

So, are you ready to budget for repairs and maintenance like a pro? If so, let's continue our journey. The path to wealth and financial freedom awaits.

Implementing Green Upgrades for Savings

As we wrap up our exploration of strategic property maintenance, let's delve into the world of green upgrades. Implementing eco-friendly improvements in your properties not only contributes to environmental sustainability but can also result in significant savings in the long run.

One of the most impactful green upgrades you can make is to improve your property's energy efficiency. This could involve installing energy-efficient appliances, upgrading to LED lighting, or adding insulation to reduce heating and cooling costs. While these upgrades may require an upfront investment, they can lead to substantial savings on utility bills over time.

Water conservation is another area where green upgrades can make a big difference. Consider installing low-flow faucets and showerheads, dual-flush toilets, or even a rainwater harvesting system. These upgrades can significantly reduce water usage, leading to lower utility bills and a smaller environmental footprint.

If you're ready to make a larger investment, consider renewable energy sources like solar panels. While the upfront cost can be significant, the long-term savings can be substantial. Plus, many states offer incentives or rebates that can offset the initial cost.

Don't forget about the potential for increased property value. Many tenants and buyers are willing to pay a premium for eco-friendly properties. By implementing green upgrades, you can make your property more attractive to these environmentally conscious individuals.

Implementing green upgrades is a win-win strategy. It's good for the environment, good for your wallet, and good for your property's value. By focusing on energy efficiency, water conservation, renewable energy, and other eco-friendly improvements, you can make your property more sustainable and cost-effective.

So, are you ready to go green and save green? If so, let's continue our journey. The path to wealth and financial freedom awaits.

Chapter 9

MASTERING THE FINANCIALS OF SECTION 8 INVESTING

Maximizing Cash Flow from Section 8 Rentals

As we embark on Chapter 9, we delve into mastering the financials of Section 8 investing. Let's kick off this chapter by discussing how to maximize cash flow from Section 8 rentals.

One of the primary advantages of investing in Section 8 housing is the potential for consistent, reliable cash flow. The government-backed rental payments can provide a steady income stream, which is a key component of successful real estate investing.

To maximize your cash flow, it's crucial to keep your properties occupied. Vacancies can significantly impact your cash flow, so it's important to minimize turnover. This can be achieved by providing a safe, clean, and comfortable living environment for your tenants, which can encourage them to stay longer.

Another key factor in maximizing cash flow is setting the right rental rate. While the Housing Authority sets a maximum allowable rent, you can still adjust your rent within this limit based on factors like the condition of the property and the local rental market. Just keep in mind that your rent must be reasonable compared to non-Section 8 rentals in the area.

Efficient property management is another crucial aspect of maximizing cash flow. This includes timely and cost-effective maintenance, effective tenant management, and efficient rent collection. By managing your properties effectively, you can reduce expenses and increase your net income.

Finally, don't overlook the importance of strategic property selection. Properties in high-demand areas can command higher rents, leading to greater cash flow. Additionally, properties with lower maintenance costs can also contribute to higher net income.

Maximizing cash flow from Section 8 rentals involves a combination of minimizing vacancies, setting the right rental rate, efficient property management, and strategic property selection. By focusing on these areas, you can optimize your cash flow and increase your return on investment.

So, are you ready to maximize your cash flow from Section 8 rentals? If so, let's continue our journey. The path to wealth and financial freedom awaits.

Tracking Your Real Estate Profits

As we continue our journey through mastering the financials of Section 8 investing, let's turn our attention to tracking your real estate profits. Understanding your financial performance is crucial in making informed decisions and planning for the future.

The first step in tracking your real estate profits is to keep detailed records of all income and expenses related to your properties. This includes not only the rental income but also expenses such as maintenance costs, property taxes, insurance premiums, and mortgage payments. It's also important to track capital expenses, such as property improvements or major repairs.

Once you have a clear picture of your income and expenses, you can calculate your net operating income (NOI). This is the income left over after subtracting all operating expenses (not including mortgage payments) from your rental income. The NOI gives you a good idea of the profitability of your property before considering debt service.

To get a complete picture of your property's profitability, you'll also need to consider your cash flow after financing. This is your NOI minus your mortgage payments. This figure gives you a true sense of how much cash your property is generating each month.

Another important metric to track is your return on investment (ROI). This is your annual profit (after all expenses and mortgage payments) divided by the amount of money you've invested in the property. ROI gives you a percentage that you can use to compare the profitability of different investments.

Don't forget about the importance of tracking property appreciation. While cash flow is important, a significant portion of your profits in real estate often comes from the property's increase in value over time. Regularly assess the value of your properties to keep track of this aspect of your profits.

Tracking your real estate profits involves keeping detailed records of income and expenses, calculating key metrics like NOI, cash flow, and ROI, and keeping track of property appreciation. By keeping a close eye on these figures, you can make informed decisions about managing your properties, making additional investments, and planning for your financial future.

So, are you ready to start tracking your real estate profits like a pro? If so, let's continue our journey. The path to wealth and financial freedom awaits.

Understanding Tax Benefits and Incentives

As we journey further into mastering the financials of Section 8 investing, let's delve into understanding tax benefits and incentives. Real estate investing offers several tax advantages that can significantly enhance your profitability if leveraged correctly.

One of the primary tax benefits of real estate investing is the ability to deduct rental expenses. This includes mortgage interest, property taxes, insurance, maintenance and repairs, property management fees, and even travel expenses related to property management. These deductions can significantly reduce your taxable income, thereby reducing your tax liability.

Another significant tax benefit is depreciation. While real estate properties typically increase in value over time, the IRS allows investors to deduct a portion of the cost of the property each year as a depreciation expense. This is a non-cash expense that can further reduce your taxable income. However, it's important to note that when you sell the property, you may have to recapture the depreciation and pay taxes on it, unless you use a strategy like a 1031 exchange to defer the tax.

Speaking of 1031 exchanges, this is another powerful tax strategy for real estate investors. Named after Section 1031 of the IRS code, this strategy allows you to defer capital gains taxes when you sell a property, as long as you reinvest the proceeds into a similar type of property within certain time limits. This can be a great way to grow your real estate portfolio while deferring taxes.

The Section 8 program also offers specific tax incentives in some areas. For example, some cities or counties offer property tax reductions or exemptions for landlords who rent to Section 8 tenants. It's worth checking with your local housing authority or a tax professional to see if such incentives are available in your area.

Lastly, it's important to understand that real estate investing offers the potential for tax-free cash flow. Because of the deductions and depreciation we discussed earlier, it's possible to have positive cash flow from a property that shows a loss for tax purposes. This means you could be receiving income from the property without owing taxes on it.

Understanding tax benefits and incentives is a crucial aspect of mastering the financials of Section 8 investing. By taking advantage of deductions, depreciation, 1031 exchanges, and other tax strategies, you can significantly enhance the profitability of your real estate investments.

So, are you ready to leverage the tax benefits of real estate investing to maximize your profits? If so, let's continue our journey. The path to wealth and financial freedom awaits.

Leveraging Depreciation and Write-Offs

As we continue to navigate the financial landscape of Section 8 investing, let's take a closer look at leveraging depreciation and write-offs. These tax strategies can significantly impact your bottom line and are a key part of mastering the financials of real estate investing.

Depreciation is a tax deduction that allows you to recover the cost of buying or improving a rental property. Essentially, it acknowledges that the physical structure of a property wears out over time and becomes less valuable. For residential real estate, the IRS typically uses a depreciation period of 27.5 years. This means that each year, you can deduct about 3.636% of the property's cost (excluding land value) from your taxable income.

To calculate your annual depreciation expense, you'll need to know your property's cost basis. This is typically the purchase price, plus any capital improvements you've made. Divide the cost basis by 27.5 to find your annual depreciation deduction. Remember, you can only depreciate the building portion of your property, not the land.

Depreciation is a powerful tax strategy because it's a non-cash expense. You don't have to spend any money to claim it, yet it can significantly reduce your taxable income. However, keep in mind that when you sell the property, you may have to recapture the depreciation, which means you'll pay tax on it at your ordinary income tax rate, unless you use a strategy like a 1031 exchange to defer the tax.

In addition to depreciation, there are many expenses you can write off as a real estate investor. These include mortgage interest, property taxes, insurance, maintenance and repairs, utilities, property management fees, and even travel expenses related to managing your properties. These write-offs can further reduce your taxable income, thereby reducing your tax liability.

One important point to remember is the difference between repairs and improvements. Repairs are necessary to keep the property in good working condition and can be deducted in the year they are incurred. Improvements add value to the property or extend its life and must be capitalized and depreciated over time.

Leveraging depreciation and write-offs is a key strategy in maximizing the profitability of your Section 8 investments. By understanding and taking advantage of these tax benefits, you can significantly reduce your tax liability and increase your cash flow.

So, are you ready to leverage depreciation and write-offs to maximize your real estate profits? If so, let's continue our journey. The path to wealth and financial freedom awaits.

Creating Long-Term Wealth through Real Estate

As we round off our exploration of mastering the financials of Section 8 investing, let's focus on the ultimate goal: creating long-term wealth through real estate. This is the end game that makes all the strategic planning, financial management, and hard work worthwhile.

Creating long-term wealth through real estate investing is not about quick flips or overnight success. It's about building a sustainable, profitable portfolio of properties that provides consistent cash flow and appreciates in value over time. It's about leveraging the power of compounding, where your wealth grows exponentially as your investments generate more income that can be reinvested.

One of the key strategies in creating long-term wealth is to reinvest your profits. This could mean using the cash flow from your existing properties to invest in more properties, or it could mean reinvesting in your existing properties to increase their value and rental income.

Another crucial strategy is to leverage the power of leverage. By using borrowed money to invest in real estate, you can control a much larger asset and benefit from its full appreciation and income potential, while only investing a fraction of the cost.

Diversification is also important in building long-term wealth. By investing in different types of properties and in different markets, you can spread your risk and increase your chances of success. The Section 8 program can be a key part of this diversification strategy, as it offers a consistent, government-backed income stream.

Finally, remember that real estate is a long-term investment. While there may be ups and downs in the market, over the long term, real estate has consistently proven to be a solid investment that appreciates in value. By staying the course and focusing on the long term, you can build substantial wealth through real estate investing.

Creating long-term wealth through real estate involves reinvesting profits, leveraging borrowed money, diversifying your investments, and focusing on the long term. By mastering these strategies, you can transform your Section 8 investments into a powerful engine of wealth creation.

So, are you ready to create long-term wealth through real estate investing? If so, let's continue our journey. The path to wealth and financial freedom awaits.

Chapter 10

SECTION 8 INSPECTIONS AND COMPLIANCE

Preparing for HUD Inspections

As we journey into Chapter 10, we delve into the world of Section 8 inspections and compliance. Let's begin with a critical aspect of this process: preparing for HUD inspections.

HUD inspections are a crucial part of the Section 8 program. The Department of Housing and Urban Development (HUD) conducts these inspections to ensure that rental properties meet the minimum standards of health and safety. As a landlord, preparing for these inspections is key to maintaining your property's eligibility for the program.

Preparation for a HUD inspection should start long before the inspector arrives. Regular maintenance and prompt attention to repair needs are crucial. This includes everything from ensuring that all electrical outlets and plumbing fixtures are working correctly to checking that smoke detectors are installed and functional.

A key aspect of HUD inspections is checking for health and safety issues. This includes things like peeling paint, which could indicate a lead hazard, or a lack of secure railings on stairs or balconies. Be proactive in addressing these issues before the inspection to avoid potential violations.

Another area that HUD inspectors focus on is the overall condition of the property. This includes the structural integrity of the building, the condition of the interior and exterior surfaces, and the functionality of the heating and plumbing systems. Regularly inspect your property and address any issues promptly to ensure it's in top shape for the HUD inspection.

It's also a good idea to familiarize yourself with the HUD's Housing Quality Standards (HQS). These are the guidelines that HUD inspectors use to assess properties. Understanding these standards can help you anticipate potential issues and address them before the inspection.

Finally, remember that preparation for a HUD inspection isn't just about passing the inspection. It's also about providing a safe, comfortable living environment for your tenants. By maintaining your property to a high standard, you can not only pass HUD inspections with ease but also attract and retain quality tenants.

Preparing for HUD inspections involves regular maintenance, prompt attention to repair needs, understanding the HUD's Housing Quality Standards, and a commitment to providing quality housing. By mastering these elements, you can navigate HUD inspections with confidence and maintain your property's eligibility for the Section 8 program.

So, are you ready to prepare for your next HUD inspection? If so, let's continue our journey. The path to wealth and financial freedom awaits.

Dealing with Inspection Failures

As we continue to navigate the world of Section 8 inspections and compliance, let's delve into dealing with inspection failures. While our goal is to pass each inspection with flying colors, there may be times when issues arise. Knowing how to handle these situations is key to maintaining your property's eligibility for the Section 8 program.

If your property fails a HUD inspection, don't panic. It's not the end of the world, and it doesn't mean you're out of the Section 8 program. It simply means there are issues that need to be addressed. The inspector will provide you with a list of the violations that need to be corrected. Review this list carefully to understand what needs to be done.

Once you've reviewed the list of violations, make a plan to address them. Prioritize the issues based on their severity and the potential impact on the tenant's health and safety. Major issues like faulty wiring or a broken heating system should be addressed immediately, while minor issues like a missing doorstop can be handled later.

Next, get to work on making the necessary repairs. Depending on the nature of the violations, you may be able to handle some repairs yourself, while others may require a professional. Be sure to keep records of all repairs, including receipts for any materials or labor. These can be helpful if there's any question about whether the issues were addressed.

After the repairs are completed, you'll need to request a re-inspection. The HUD inspector will come back to the property to verify that all violations have been corrected. If all issues have been addressed, the property will pass the inspection and remain eligible for the Section 8 program.

If the property fails the re-inspection, you'll need to repeat the process. It's crucial to address all violations and ensure the property meets HUD's Housing Quality Standards. Continued failures can result in the property being removed from the Section 8 program, so it's in your best interest to address any issues promptly and thoroughly.

Dealing with inspection failures involves understanding the violations, making a plan to address them, completing the necessary repairs, and requesting a re-inspection. By handling these situations promptly and effectively, you can keep your property in compliance with the Section 8 program and maintain your steady stream of rental income.

So, are you ready to tackle any inspection failures that come your way? If so, let's continue our journey. The path to wealth and financial freedom awaits.

Building Relationships with Inspectors

As we further explore Section 8 inspections and compliance, let's shift our focus to building relationships with inspectors. This may seem like a minor detail in the grand scheme of real estate investing, but cultivating positive relationships with the people who inspect your properties can have significant benefits.

First, let's dispel any notion that inspectors are the enemy. They're not. They are professionals doing their job, which is to ensure that rental properties meet the minimum standards of health and safety. They play a crucial role in the Section 8 program, and as a landlord, it's in your best interest to work with them, not against them.

Building a positive relationship with inspectors starts with respect. Respect their time by being prepared for inspections. Have all necessary paperwork ready, ensure that the property is clean and accessible, and be on time for the inspection. If you're unable to be there in person, have a reliable representative present.

Communication is key. If there are issues with the property that you're aware of, be upfront about them. If you're in the process of making repairs, let the inspector know. They will appreciate your honesty and your commitment to maintaining your property to a high standard.

Be open to feedback. If the inspector points out issues that need to be addressed, don't get defensive. Instead, see it as valuable information that can help you improve your property and keep it in compliance with HUD's Housing Quality Standards.

Remember, inspectors have a wealth of knowledge about property maintenance and HUD regulations. Use this to your advantage. Ask questions, seek advice, and learn from their expertise. This not only helps you maintain your property, but it also shows the inspector that you're serious about being a responsible landlord.

Finally, keep in mind that building relationships takes time. Be patient, be consistent, and be professional. Over time, you'll establish a positive rapport with the inspectors, which can make the inspection process smoother and more efficient.

Building relationships with inspectors is an often overlooked but important aspect of Section 8 investing. By showing respect, communicating effectively, being open to feedback, and leveraging the inspector's expertise, you can cultivate positive relationships that benefit your real estate business.

So, are you ready to start building relationships with inspectors? If so, let's continue our journey. The path to wealth and financial freedom awaits.

Keeping Your Properties Compliant Year-Round

As we continue our journey through Section 8 inspections and compliance, let's focus on keeping your properties compliant year-round. This is a critical aspect of being a successful Section 8 landlord, as it ensures your properties remain eligible for the program and avoids any interruptions to your rental income.

Keeping your properties compliant year-round starts with understanding HUD's Housing Quality Standards (HQS). These are the minimum health and safety standards that rental properties must meet to be eligible for the Section 8 program. Familiarize yourself with these standards and use them as a guide for maintaining your properties.

Regular property inspections are a key part of keeping your properties compliant. Don't wait for the annual HUD inspection to find out about issues. Instead, conduct your own inspections periodically to catch and address problems early. This not only keeps your properties in compliance but also helps prevent small issues from becoming major problems.

Maintenance is another crucial aspect of keeping your properties compliant. This includes routine maintenance like changing air filters and servicing HVAC systems, as well as addressing repair needs promptly. Remember, as a landlord, you're responsible for maintaining the property in a habitable condition. This means ensuring that all systems are functioning properly and that the property is safe and clean.

When it comes to repairs, don't cut corners. Use quality materials and hire reputable contractors. This not only ensures that the repairs are done correctly but also helps maintain the value and longevity of your property. Keep records of all repairs and maintenance activities. These can be useful for tax purposes and can also provide evidence of compliance in case of a dispute.

Finally, keep open lines of communication with your tenants. Encourage them to report any issues promptly and respond to their concerns in a timely manner. Remember, your tenants are your eyes and ears on the property. They can alert you to potential problems that you may not be aware of.

Keeping your properties compliant year-round involves understanding HUD's Housing Quality Standards, conducting regular property inspections, maintaining and repairing your properties, and communicating effectively with your tenants. By mastering these elements, you can ensure your properties remain eligible for the Section 8 program and maintain a steady stream of rental income.

So, are you ready to keep your properties compliant year-round? If so, let's continue our journey. The path to wealth and financial freedom awaits.

Handling Emergency Repairs

As we round off our exploration of Section 8 inspections and compliance, let's delve into handling emergency repairs. This is an inevitable part of being a landlord, and knowing how to handle these situations effectively is crucial to maintaining your property's compliance and ensuring the safety and satisfaction of your tenants.

Emergency repairs can range from a broken heating system in the middle of winter to a burst water pipe that's causing flooding. These are issues that pose a serious risk to the health and safety of your tenants and need to be addressed immediately.

When an emergency repair situation arises, the first step is to assess the situation. Determine the severity of the issue and the potential risk to the tenant. If necessary, arrange for the tenant to temporarily vacate the property until the issue is resolved.

Next, contact a reputable contractor to handle the repair. It's a good idea to have a list of trusted contractors that you can call on in an emergency. Make sure they're licensed and insured, and that they have experience with the type of repair needed.

While the repair is being done, keep the lines of communication open with your tenant. Keep them updated on the progress of the repair and give them an estimated timeline for when they can expect the issue to be resolved. This can help alleviate their stress and show them that you're taking the issue seriously.

Once the repair is completed, inspect the work to ensure it's been done properly. Also, follow up with your tenant to make sure they're satisfied with the repair and that there are no further issues.

Handling emergency repairs involves assessing the situation, contacting a reputable contractor, communicating with your tenant, and inspecting the completed work. By handling these situations promptly and effectively, you can maintain your property's compliance, ensure the safety of your tenants, and preserve your relationship with them.

So, are you ready to handle any emergency repairs that come your way? If so, let's continue our journey. The path to wealth and financial freedom awaits.

Chapter 11

EXIT STRATEGIES AND LONG-TERM PLANNING

When to Sell Your Section 8 Properties

As we venture into Chapter 11, we shift our focus to exit strategies and long-term planning. A key part of this is knowing when to sell your Section 8 properties. This decision can have significant implications for your real estate investing journey and your overall financial goals.

Deciding when to sell a Section 8 property is not a decision to be taken lightly. It requires careful consideration of several factors, including market conditions, the performance of the property, and your long-term investment goals.

Market conditions play a significant role in the decision to sell. If property values are on the rise and you can get a good price for your property, it may be a good time to sell. However, if the market is in a slump and property values are low, it might be better to hold onto the property and wait for conditions to improve.

The performance of the property is another important factor. If the property is consistently generating a good return on investment, it may be worth holding onto. However, if the property is underperforming or has become a financial burden, selling may be the best option.

Your long-term investment goals should also guide your decision. If you're looking to scale up and invest in larger properties, selling a smaller property could provide the capital you need. On the other hand, if you're looking to simplify your portfolio or transition to more passive investments, selling could be a step in the right direction.

It's also important to consider the impact of selling on your tenants. The Section 8 program provides much-needed housing for low-income families, and selling a property could potentially disrupt their living situation. Be sure to consider the human element in your decision and do what you can to minimize any negative impact on your tenants.

Deciding when to sell your Section 8 properties involves careful consideration of market conditions, property performance, your long-term investment goals, and the impact on your tenants. By weighing these factors and making a strategic decision, you can maximize your profits and continue to progress towards your financial goals.

So, are you ready to make strategic decisions about when to sell your Section 8 properties? If so, let's continue our journey. The path to wealth and financial freedom awaits.

Selling Your Portfolio for Maximum Profit

As we continue our exploration of exit strategies and long-term planning, let's delve into selling your portfolio for maximum profit. This is a crucial aspect of real estate investing, and knowing how to navigate this process can significantly impact your financial success.

Selling your portfolio for maximum profit involves several key steps. The first is to assess the value of your portfolio. This involves evaluating the current market value of your properties, considering factors such as location, property condition, and rental income. You may want to enlist the help of a real estate appraiser or agent to ensure you get an accurate valuation.

Next, consider the timing of the sale. As with individual properties, market conditions can significantly impact the profit you can make from selling your portfolio. If property values are high and demand is strong, it may be a good time to sell. However, if the market is weak, it might be better to hold onto your portfolio until conditions improve.

Once you've decided to sell, you'll need to prepare your portfolio for sale. This might involve making repairs or upgrades to increase property values, ensuring all properties are fully tenanted to show strong rental income, and getting your financial records in order to demonstrate the profitability of your portfolio.

Marketing your portfolio effectively is also crucial. This could involve listing your properties on real estate websites, networking with other investors, or working with a real estate agent who specializes in investment properties. Highlight the strengths of your portfolio, such as consistent rental income, good property condition, and desirable location.

Finally, be prepared to negotiate. Potential buyers will likely want to negotiate the price, terms, and conditions of the sale. Be clear about your bottom line and be prepared to walk away if a deal doesn't meet your needs.

Selling your portfolio for maximum profit involves assessing the value of your portfolio, considering the timing of the sale, preparing your portfolio for sale, marketing effectively, and negotiating the deal. By mastering these steps, you can maximize your profits and make a successful exit from your real estate investments.

So, are you ready to sell your portfolio for maximum profit? If so, let's continue our journey. The path to wealth and financial freedom awaits.

Tax Planning for Property Sales

As we delve deeper into exit strategies and long-term planning, we now turn our attention to tax planning for property sales. This is a critical aspect of real estate investing that can significantly impact your profits and overall financial health.

When you sell a property, you're typically required to pay capital gains tax on the profit you make from the sale. This is calculated by subtracting the cost of purchasing and improving the property from the sale price. The resulting gain is then subject to capital gains tax.

However, there are strategies you can use to minimize or even eliminate your capital gains tax liability. One of these is the use of a

1031 exchange. This IRS provision allows you to defer paying capital gains tax if you reinvest the profits from the sale into a like-kind property. This can be a powerful tool for growing your real estate portfolio while deferring taxes.

Another strategy is to take advantage of the depreciation recapture tax break. This allows you to offset the capital gains from the sale with the depreciation you've claimed on the property over the years. However, it's important to note that if you sell the property for more than its depreciated value, you may have to pay depreciation recapture tax.

You can also offset your capital gains with capital losses from other investments. If you've sold other properties or investments at a loss, you can use these losses to offset your gains and reduce your tax liability.

It's also important to consider the impact of the sale on your income tax. The profit from the sale could push you into a higher tax bracket, increasing your overall tax liability. You may want to consider strategies to spread out the income from the sale over multiple years to avoid a significant increase in your income tax.

Finally, consider working with a tax professional who specializes in real estate. They can help you navigate the complex tax laws and regulations and develop a tax planning strategy that maximizes your profits and minimizes your tax liability.

Tax planning for property sales involves understanding capital gains tax, utilizing tax-deferred strategies like the 1031 exchange, taking advantage of depreciation recapture, offsetting gains with losses, managing the impact on your income tax, and working with a tax professional. By mastering these strategies, you can maximize your profits and make a successful exit from your real estate investments.

So, are you ready to navigate the complexities of tax planning for property sales? If so, let's continue our journey. The path to wealth and financial freedom awaits.

Transitioning from Active to Passive Investing

As we continue our journey through exit strategies and long-term planning, let's shift our focus to transitioning from active to passive investing. This is a significant step in the real estate investing journey and one that can provide you with more freedom and flexibility.

Active investing, such as buying, renovating, and managing properties, can be time-consuming and labor-intensive. It involves a hands-on approach and requires a significant amount of effort and involvement. On the other hand, passive investing allows you to earn income from real estate with less direct involvement.

The transition from active to passive investing is not a decision to be taken lightly. It requires careful planning and strategic decision-making. Here are some key steps to consider in this transition.

First, assess your current portfolio. Consider the performance of each property and the amount of time and effort required to manage it. This will help you determine which properties to hold onto and which to sell as you transition to a more passive investment strategy.

Next, consider your financial goals. Passive investing often provides a slower but more steady income stream. It's important to ensure that this aligns with your financial goals and lifestyle preferences. For example, if you're nearing retirement, the steady income from passive investments may be more appealing.

One popular form of passive investing is investing in real estate investment trusts (REITs). These are companies that own, operate, or finance income-generating real estate. By investing in a REIT, you can earn income from real estate without the need to buy or manage properties yourself.

Another option is to invest in real estate syndications or funds. These are pooled investment vehicles where multiple investors come together to invest in larger real estate projects. This can provide access to larger, more profitable deals that you might not be able to invest in individually.

You could also consider hiring a property management company to manage your properties. This can free up your time while still allowing you to reap the benefits of property ownership.

Finally, it's important to educate yourself about passive investing. Read books, attend seminars, and network with other investors. The more you know, the better equipped you'll be to make informed decisions.

Transitioning from active to passive investing involves assessing your portfolio, considering your financial goals, exploring passive investment options, and educating yourself about passive investing. By taking these steps, you can transition smoothly and successfully from active to passive investing, providing you with more freedom and potentially more consistent income.

So, are you ready to make the transition from active to passive investing? If so, let's continue our journey. The path to wealth and financial freedom awaits.

Leaving a Legacy: Building Wealth for Generations

As we conclude our exploration of exit strategies and long-term planning, let's delve into one of the most rewarding aspects of real estate investing: leaving a legacy and building wealth for generations. This is the ultimate goal for many investors, and it's a testament to the power and potential of real estate as a wealth-building tool.

Building wealth for generations involves more than just amassing a large portfolio of properties. It's about creating a sustainable and scalable system that can continue to generate income and grow in value over time. It's about setting up structures and strategies that can be passed down to your children and grandchildren, providing them with financial security and opportunities for their own wealth creation.

One way to do this is by setting up a real estate holding company or a trust to manage your properties. This not only provides a legal structure for your investments but also allows for easier transition of assets to your heirs. It can also provide tax benefits and protect your assets from potential liabilities.

Education is another crucial component of leaving a legacy. Teach your children and grandchildren about real estate investing. Share your knowledge and experiences with them. Encourage them to learn about finance, economics, and real estate. This can equip them with the skills and knowledge they need to manage and grow the wealth you've built.

Finally, remember that leaving a legacy is not just about wealth. It's also about values. Instill in your descendants the values that have guided your investing journey, such as hard work, patience, resilience, and integrity. These values, combined with the financial legacy you leave, can empower them to build their own wealth and, in turn, leave their own legacy.

Building wealth for generations involves setting up legal structures for your investments, educating your descendants about real estate investing, and instilling in them the values that have guided your journey. By doing this, you can leave a legacy that extends beyond your lifetime, benefiting your family for generations to come.

So, are you ready to build a legacy that lasts? If so, let's continue our journey. The path to wealth and financial freedom awaits.

Chapter 12

STREET-SMART TIPS FOR SECTION 8 LANDLORDS

Safety Tips for Working in High-Crime Areas

As we embark on Chapter 12, we delve into the street-smart tips for Section 8 landlords. One of the realities of investing in Section 8 housing is that you may often find yourself working in high-crime areas. This can be daunting, but with the right approach and precautions, you can ensure your safety while effectively managing your properties.

First and foremost, it's crucial to familiarize yourself with the area. Understand the neighborhood dynamics, know the hotspots for crime, and be aware of the times when crime rates are typically high. This knowledge will help you plan your visits to the property at safer times and avoid potential trouble spots.

When visiting your properties, always let someone know where you're going and when you expect to return. This could be a family member, a friend, or a team member. In case of any unforeseen circumstances, someone should know your whereabouts.

Consider investing in personal safety equipment. This could include items like pepper spray, a personal alarm, or even a bulletproof vest if you feel it's necessary. Remember, your safety is paramount, and it's better to be over-prepared than under-prepared.

Always maintain a professional demeanor and appearance when interacting with tenants or others in the neighborhood. Avoid displaying signs of wealth such as expensive jewelry or luxury cars, as this could make you a target. Treat everyone with respect and maintain a firm but fair approach in all interactions.

Finally, build relationships with local law enforcement. They can provide valuable insights into the area's crime trends and offer advice on staying safe. If you're regularly in the area, they'll get to know you, which can be beneficial in case of any issues.

Ensuring your safety in high-crime areas involves familiarizing yourself with the area, letting someone know your whereabouts, investing in personal safety equipment, maintaining a professional demeanor, and building relationships with local law enforcement. By taking these precautions, you can navigate these areas safely while effectively managing your Section 8 properties.

So, are you ready to navigate high-crime areas with confidence and ensure your safety? If so, let's continue our journey. The path to wealth and financial freedom awaits.

Playing Fair but Firm with Tenants

As we delve deeper into Chapter 12, let's shift our focus to a critical aspect of being a Section 8 landlord: playing fair but firm with tenants. This balance is crucial in maintaining a successful landlord-tenant relationship and ensuring the smooth operation of your rental properties.

Being a landlord, especially in the Section 8 program, requires a delicate balance of fairness and firmness. Your tenants are individuals who deserve respect and understanding. However, you also have a business to run and rules to enforce. Striking this balance can be challenging, but it's essential for success.

Firstly, it's crucial to treat all tenants with respect and dignity. Remember, they are not just a source of income; they are people with their own lives, challenges, and needs. Treat them as you would want to be treated and always communicate in a respectful and professional manner.

At the same time, you must enforce the rules and regulations of your rental agreement. This includes timely rent payments, property maintenance, and adherence to any property rules. If a tenant fails to meet these obligations, you must address the issue promptly and firmly.

When dealing with issues, it's important to be fair but firm. If a tenant is consistently late with rent, for example, you need to address the issue. However, if they are facing a temporary hardship and have generally been a good tenant, you might consider working out a temporary payment plan rather than immediately resorting to eviction.

Documenting all interactions with your tenants is also crucial. This includes everything from rent payments to complaints or issues raised by the tenant. Having a record of all interactions can protect you in case of disputes or legal issues down the line.

It's also important to stay up-to-date on landlord-tenant laws in your area. These laws can vary widely, and failing to adhere to them can result in legal issues and financial penalties. Make sure you understand your rights and responsibilities as a landlord, as well as the rights and protections afforded to your tenants.

Finally, don't be afraid to seek professional advice when needed. Whether it's a lawyer, a property management company, or a fellow landlord, having a network of professionals you can turn to for advice can be invaluable.

Playing fair but firm with tenants involves treating them with respect, enforcing rules and regulations, addressing issues promptly, documenting all interactions, understanding landlord-tenant laws, and seeking professional advice when needed. By mastering these strategies, you can maintain a successful landlord-tenant relationship and ensure the smooth operation of your rental properties.

So, are you ready to strike the balance of playing fair but firm with your tenants? If so, let's continue our journey. The path to wealth and financial freedom awaits.

Dealing with Difficult Inspectors and Bureaucrats

As we continue our journey through Chapter 12, let's tackle a challenging aspect of Section 8 investing: dealing with difficult inspectors and bureaucrats. This is an inevitable part of participating in a government program, but with the right strategies, you can navigate these interactions effectively and maintain a successful investment.

Firstly, it's crucial to understand the role of inspectors and bureaucrats in the Section 8 program. Inspectors are responsible for ensuring that your property meets the Housing Quality Standards set by the Department of Housing and Urban Development (HUD). Bureaucrats, on the other hand, manage the administrative aspects of the program, such as tenant applications and rent payments.

When dealing with inspectors, preparation is key. Ensure your property is in top condition before the inspection. Familiarize yourself with the HUD standards and address any potential issues beforehand. This not only increases your chances of passing the inspection but also demonstrates your commitment to maintaining quality housing.

However, even with preparation, you may encounter inspectors who are particularly strict or difficult. In such cases, it's important to remain professional and respectful. Listen to their concerns, ask for clarification if needed, and address any issues promptly. If you disagree with an inspector's findings, you can request a review or appeal through the proper channels.

Dealing with bureaucrats can also be challenging, particularly when it comes to navigating the administrative complexities of the Section 8 program. Here, patience and persistence are your allies. Be prepared for potential delays and bureaucratic red tape. Keep all your documents organized and readily available to facilitate the process.

Communication is also crucial when dealing with bureaucrats. Be clear and concise in your communications, whether it's in person, over the phone, or via email. If you're unsure about something, don't hesitate to ask for clarification. Misunderstandings can lead to delays or complications, so it's better to ask questions upfront.

Remember, bureaucrats are people too, and they're often dealing with a high workload and strict regulations. A little kindness and understanding can go a long way in building a positive relationship.

In situations where you're facing significant difficulties or roadblocks, don't hesitate to seek professional help. This could be a lawyer, a property management company, or a real estate professional experienced in Section 8 investing. Their expertise can be invaluable in navigating complex situations.

Dealing with difficult inspectors and bureaucrats involves preparation, professionalism, patience, clear communication, and seeking professional help when needed. These strategies can help you navigate the complexities of the Section 8 program and maintain a successful investment.

So, are you ready to tackle the challenge of dealing with difficult inspectors and bureaucrats? If so, let's continue our journey. The path to wealth and financial freedom awaits.

Handling Legal Challenges and Court Cases

As we progress through Chapter 12, we now turn our attention to a potentially daunting aspect of being a Section 8 landlord: handling legal challenges and court cases. While it's not a pleasant topic, it's a reality that landlords may face, and being prepared can make all the difference.

Firstly, prevention is the best approach. This starts with a thorough understanding of landlord-tenant laws in your area, which can vary widely. Knowing these laws can help you avoid potential legal pitfalls and ensure you're treating your tenants fairly and legally. This includes understanding eviction laws, security deposit regulations, and the rights and protections afforded to tenants.

A solid lease agreement is another preventative measure. This document should clearly outline the rights and responsibilities of both parties. It should include details on rent payments, property maintenance, and the procedures for addressing issues or disputes. A well-drafted lease can provide legal protection and serve as a reference point in case of disagreements.

Despite your best efforts, you may still find yourself facing a legal challenge. This could be a dispute with a tenant, a disagreement with an inspector, or a lawsuit. In these situations, it's crucial to stay calm and approach the situation methodically.

Document everything. This includes all interactions with the tenant, inspector, or bureaucrat, as well as any actions taken. These records can be invaluable in presenting your case and defending your actions.

Seek legal advice. If you're facing a serious legal challenge, it's wise to consult with a lawyer, preferably one who specializes in real estate or landlord-tenant law. They can provide guidance, represent you if necessary, and help you navigate the legal process.

If the case goes to court, be prepared. Gather all your documents, consult with your lawyer, and be ready to present your case clearly and professionally. Remember, the court is there to ensure justice and fairness, so be honest, respectful, and prepared.

Finally, learn from the experience. Legal challenges can be stressful and costly, but they can also provide valuable lessons. Use these experiences to improve your practices, revise your lease agreement, or update your tenant screening process.

Handling legal challenges and court cases involves understanding the law, having a solid lease agreement, documenting everything, seeking legal advice, being prepared for court, and learning from the experience. By mastering these strategies, you can handle legal challenges confidently and effectively, ensuring the success and sustainability of your Section 8 investments.

So, are you ready to tackle legal challenges and court cases with confidence? If so, let's continue our journey. The path to wealth and financial freedom awaits.

The Long Game: Lessons from a Veteran Investor

As we draw near the end of Chapter 12, let's delve into the long game: lessons from a veteran investor. Real estate investing, particularly in Section 8 housing, is not a get-rich-quick scheme. It's a long-term endeavor that requires patience, persistence, and a strategic approach.

Over the years, I've learned that success in real estate investing is about more than just buying properties and collecting rent. It's about understanding the market, building relationships, managing risks, and constantly learning and adapting.

Understanding the market is crucial. This includes not only the real estate market but also the broader economic trends that can impact it. Stay informed about changes in housing policies, interest rates, and local economic conditions. This will help you make informed investment decisions and anticipate potential challenges.

Building relationships is another key aspect of the long game. This includes relationships with tenants, inspectors, bureaucrats, and other real estate professionals. These relationships can provide valuable insights, facilitate your operations, and open up new opportunities.

Risk management is a critical part of real estate investing. This involves diversifying your portfolio, maintaining adequate insurance, and staying compliant with all laws and regulations. It also involves planning for unexpected events, such as vacancies, maintenance issues, or changes in the market.

Continuous learning and adaptation are what separate successful investors from the rest. The real estate market is constantly evolving, and so should your strategies. Attend seminars, read books, network with other investors, and stay open to new ideas and approaches.

Finally, remember to enjoy the journey. Real estate investing can be challenging, but it can also be incredibly rewarding. Celebrate your successes, learn from your failures, and always keep your eye on the long-term goal: building wealth and financial freedom.

The long game in real estate investing involves understanding the market, building relationships, managing risks, continuous learning and adaptation, and enjoying the journey. These lessons, learned over many years as a veteran investor, can guide you towards success in your own real estate investing journey.

So, are you ready to play the long game and build lasting wealth through real estate investing? If so, let's continue our journey. The path to wealth and financial freedom awaits.

CONCLUSION

As we reach the conclusion of our journey through the world of Section 8 investing, it's time to look ahead. The future of Section 8 investing is promising, with the demand for affordable housing showing no signs of slowing down. The government's commitment to providing safe, decent, and affordable housing for low-income families means that the Section 8 program is likely to continue playing a significant role in the housing market.

However, as with any investment, it's important to stay adaptable. Market conditions, housing policies, and economic factors can change, and successful investors are those who can adapt their strategies to these changes. This might mean exploring new markets, adjusting your property management strategies, or diversifying your portfolio. The key is to stay informed, stay flexible, and always be ready to seize new opportunities.

Adaptability also extends to dealing with the challenges that come with being a Section 8 landlord. Whether it's navigating the complexities of the program, dealing with difficult tenants, or handling legal issues, being able to adapt and find solutions is crucial. Remember, challenges are part of the journey, and overcoming them is what makes you a stronger and more successful investor.

Now, let's talk about your path to financial freedom. Real estate investing, particularly in Section 8 housing, offers a unique opportunity to build wealth and achieve financial independence. The consistent, government-backed income can provide a stable foundation for your investment portfolio, while the potential for property appreciation can boost your long-term wealth.

But remember, real estate investing is not a get-rich-quick scheme. It's a long-term endeavor that requires patience, persistence, and strategic planning. It's about playing the long game, staying committed through the ups and downs, and always keeping your eye on the ultimate goal: financial freedom.

So, as we conclude this book, I want to leave you with a few final thoughts. First, I hope that this book has provided you with valuable insights and practical strategies for succeeding in Section 8 investing. But more than that, I hope it has inspired you to take action. Knowledge is valuable, but it's the application of that knowledge that leads to success.

Second, remember that your journey as a real estate investor is unique. Your path may not look exactly like mine or anyone else's, and that's okay. What matters is that you're taking steps towards your goals, learning from your experiences, and making progress in your own way.

And finally, I want to remind you that you're not alone in this journey. There's a community of real estate investors out there, each with their own experiences, insights, and lessons to share. I encourage you to connect with this community, whether it's through networking events, online forums, or local real estate clubs. The support, advice, and camaraderie you'll find can be invaluable.

The future of Section 8 investing is promising, but it requires adaptability, strategic planning, and a long-term view. Your path to financial freedom through real estate investing is a unique journey, filled with challenges, triumphs, and valuable lessons. But remember, you're not alone, and with the right strategies, persistence, and a supportive community, you can achieve your goals and enjoy the rewards of financial freedom.

So, are you ready to embark on your own journey in Section 8 investing? If so, I wish you all the best. The path to wealth and financial freedom awaits. Let's get started!

Made in the USA
Columbia, SC
27 January 2025